Beautiful
ROSES

"A rose would be only half a rose

if it did not have a fragrance."

Alphonse Karr (1808–1890)

Beautiful
ROSES

Marie-Hélène Loaëc

Photography by Jacques Boulay

STERLING PUBLISHING CO., INC.

NEW YORK

Contents

The Pleasures of the Senses

"God gave to the rose the luster of the most

sparkling metal and the scent of the sweetest

of perfumes. The rose offers the brilliant colors

of the rainbow and sends the most learned

into confusion; because they cannot say if a

cup filled with crimson-colored wine and

wreathed with roses gives them its splendor or

receives it from them."

The Thousand and One Nights—14th Century

What is more natural, before a budding or full-bloomed rose in a garden or a vase, than to bring our noses to it to discover its fragrance? And when it has none, aren't we a bit disappointed, as if a dimension of our pleasure is lost?

The rose is one of those flowers that excites not only the sight but also the sense of smell. It is this sense, probably the least developed, which has the greatest power to stir the memory, to move us back as far as childhood. Close your eyes, let yourself drift back to a memory retrieved by a scent…and happiness is there, ineffable.

"A rose without perfume is only half a rose," the writer and journalist Alphonse Karr delighted in saying in the 1800s. Many enthusiasts today share his opinion: the pleasure is not complete unless the rose you admire is fragrant. This is the case with the 'James Pereire,' a recent creation of Meilland (page 8).

To take a flower in the hollow of your hand, to caress it gently also brings pleasing and nuanced sensations: the petals are thin and silky or thicker and more substantial, the grasp on the flower firm or loose, the shape perceptible, flat or large ball. Be careful of the thorns, though; they are there to protect it….

As for taste, it has that too…certain drinks and recipes remind us that the petals of the rose can also tempt the taste buds.

All that is left to satisfy is the hearing. A soft breeze or a bit of birdsong or well-chosen classical music could round out the sensations with sound.

The large family of roses

Surely nothing has a history as complicated as roses, for under the single genus Rosa, there are many species scattered throughout the world.

The rose appeared on the Earth long before human beings, at least 12 million years ago—20 million, according to some—although the fossils discovered were not, strictly speaking, roses. What is certain is that the genus lived naturally throughout the entire Northern Hemisphere, and botanists estimate from 100 to 200 species of roses grew in the temperate and tropical regions of Europe, North America, North Africa, and Asia.

The voyages of explorers and the work of botanists have further helped to distribute these different species of Rosa from one end of the Earth to the other. They have been carefully studied, artistically rendered, passionately cultivated, and moreover, crossed with one another in order to bring out those qualities which were most appreciated by enthusiasts of each era, generation after generation. There are so many species names—according to origin, hybridization, or the regions most famous for their growth—that even the most highly skilled specialists have difficulty establishing an absolute classification.

Today, catalogs, guides, and articles dedicated to the large family of roses distinguish broad groupings by the shape of the shrub and the arrangement of the flowers.

Large-flowered rose bushes produce the most majestic roses, with a diameter of 3 to 5 inches (9 to 13 cm), which are usually the most fragrant. These bushes, which reach from 24 inches to 60 inches (60 to 150 cm), are described as either Hybrid Teas, when the stems bear a single flower, or Grandiflora, when there are many, up to five or six. These are the roses that include in their ancestry the famous tea-scented roses brought from China in the 19th century.

Roses bring to a bouquet a precious and refined note, even more appreciated when, in addition to being beautiful, they are deliciously fragrant!

The clustered-flower rose bushes join from five to six, and sometimes up to a dozen, smaller roses, of about 1.5 to 3.5 inches (4 to 9 cm) in diameter, grouped in inflorescences. These flowers can have many petals or only five around a heart of stamen, as in simple eglantines (i.e., wild roses or dog-roses).

The inflorescences form clusters of flowers that cover the shrubs during the summer. Unfortunately for lovers of fragrant roses,

none of these really gives off a remarkable scent. This group includes those roses once distinguished as Floribundas and Polyanthas, the latter presenting the thickest inflorescences of slightly smaller flowers.

Landscaping roses, with erect, slightly cascading vegetation, join shrubs and ground covers as veritable rambling roses that spread out on the ground. They are generally robust and very prolific bloomers and need only minor care for truly spectacular results. Not prone to disease, they keep an attractive natural bearing requiring almost no pruning and form large clusters or wild hedges that beautify slopes and hard-to-reach corners.

On the down side, these pleasant and easy-to-grow roses are rarely, in fact almost never, fragrant

Climbing roses, also called Rambling roses, develop long branches that must be trained, making them ideal to cover a support: a pergola or trellis, a pylon, dead tree, or gutter...unless they are fortunate enough to grow on the side of a house. These varieties are mutations of those rose bushes with this same natural growth tendency. There's no surprise then in finding in this family many beautifully scented varieties with a decided plus: the perfume is at nose level, without having to stoop down.

Miniature roses have a small growth, no more than 20 inches (50 cm), and bear small flowers of an inch to an inch and a half (2 to 4 cm) in diameter. They cultivate very well in pots and can adorn balconies, terraces, windowsills, or even rooms inside the house. In the garden, they also have a place, forming low clusters, decorating borders or accenting a rock garden. Grafted on a stem, they form lovely little rose trees with multiple uses. Their cut flowers are ideal for table decorations. But there, once again, the charm of these small roses never adds more than a hint of fragrance.

Fragrant roses: a timeless seduction

In the 8th century B.C., Homer was already recounting how Aphrodite covered the body of Hector with rose oil obtained by soaking the petals in olive oil. The poet Sappho at the beginning of the 7th century B.C. had awarded the rose the title, "The Queen of Flowers." And Herodotus, two centuries later, told how King Midas loved the roses in his garden.

For many enthusiasts, there is no greater perfection in the world of flowers than a rose in full bloom. Whether they blossom in the garden or decorate the house, they merit the name, "The Queen of Flowers." Such is 'Léonidas,' a beautiful and very recent creation of Meilland, a bouquet rose of exceptional color.

The passion for roses goes back beyond the mists of time, and tales of the rose are many, as are descriptions and drawings. Roses have even been the stars of commercial catalogs for over a century.

Roses are so varied in the arrangement of their petals, the shades of their colors, and the evolution of their shape that they are for the enthusiast a continual enchantment, a discovery that is always new.

For the Romans, roses were continuously present in daily life. Pliny the Elder especially told how the mistresses of the house incorporated them into fancy dishes and plucked their petals into cups of wine, while the servants perfumed baths and pools with them. On the days of festival, their petals were strewn in the streets in enormous quantities.

The Romans imported roses by the boatload before establishing their own means of cultivation.

In the first centuries of the Common Era, roses in the Middle East were reserved for pharmaceutical use. The Persian city, Chiraz, acquired fame for the rose water distilled there from the flower's petals, beginning in the 8th century. For nearly a thousand years this rose water was exported to Europe, India, and China. The Persian sultans carried the refinement so far as to decorate their mattresses with the precious petals.

The Crusades brought the first roses to France, causing a craze there with the beauty of their flowers and their fragrance. And the specialists of the era discovered that it was possible, by blending the species, to create new roses with even more outstanding qualities. Many documents from the 17th century remain, showing the varietal creations of the horticulturists of the era: their roses

offered only a limited palette of colors—white, pink, red—but they were, for the most part, deliciously perfumed.

As it did in the Orient, the rose has made itself a flower highly prized by perfume makers since the Renaissance. It found many uses: to scent leather gloves, to prepare jams and pastes, to make rose oil, rose water, and most importantly, rose essence—to which was given medicinal value. The small city of Provins, in France, had at that time a strategic location and the rose made its fortune.

It wasn't until the second half of the 18th century, a little over two hundred years ago, that roses came veritably to besiege gardens for their decorative qualities, before becoming truly popular in the 19th century.

Roses are hermaphrodites: they combine in a single flower the male and female reproductive organs. In nature they self-fertilize—wind and insects bring the pollen from one flower to the pistils of its neighbors.

For centuries, rose growers tinkered with nature by manually inducing the fertilization of a rose with another species or variety. Even before Gregor Mendel advanced his theory of heredity in 1865 and the relative roles of dominant and recessive characteristics were understood, rose growers knew they could also produce new varieties and transmit certain characteristics from two parent roses to their descendants. They had only to select the most interesting results and reproduce them according to the traditional methods of cultivation.

Today, rose hybridizers continue this practice, but under much more rigorous scientific conditions. With thousands of varieties at their disposal, they partner "fathers" and "mothers," the first generally bearing the characteristics of color and fragrance and the latter generally bearing the morphology, or shape. These multiple

The rose enhances a bouquet like no other flower, lending a charm from sophisticated to totally natural.

Small wild roses emit their fragrance perhaps only to attract insects, which are necessary to their reproduction. What bliss these rose growers enjoy who have patiently, over centuries, bred for this characteristic, solely for the pleasure it provides.

hybridizations give birth to the seeds that will be sewn the next year. The study of these little plants culminates with the retention of 2 to 3% of interesting subjects, and each successive year entails an increasingly stringent selection. It is not until after eight to ten years of meticulous labor that the grower is even able to offer to enthusiasts those new roses he considers the most deserving.

New varieties can also appear by natural mutation of existing roses. The growth habit of the plant especially can change: this is how climbing roses appeared from rose bushes. Among the fifty most beautiful fragrant roses collected here, some are suggested under both forms, bush and climbing.

[Roses of great fragrance]

The picking of roses intended for perfume making is a delicate operation: at the very beginning of day, the flowers are richest in volatile products, i.e., their perfume. So it is carried out at dawn, from flower to flower, as quickly as possible. Once warmed by the

sun, they give off a much stronger but less sweet scent.

The flowers are harvested by hand. A good worker gathers between 11 to 17 pounds (5 and 8 kg) of petals an hour, which will yield…one tiny fraction of an ounce (1 g) of precious rose essence. No less than two and a half tons of flowers are needed to obtain a pound of it! In Grasse, France, more than 300 tons of roses are produced each year solely for this industry.

In perfumery, from among the hundreds of known species of roses, only two botanical varieties are used: the *Rosa centifolia*, also called the rose of May or the rose of Provence, and the *Rosa x damascena*, or the rose of Damascus. The *centifolia* grows in Grasse on the Côte d'Azur and in Morocco and the *damascena* is cultivated in Bulgaria, Rumania and Turkey.

Each is treated differently: (1) the *Rosa centifolia* of Grasse gives an absolute essence through extraction by volatile solvents; (2) the *Rosa x damascena* of Bulgaria is treated only with water vapor: and (3) the *Rosa centifolia* of Morocco and the *Rosa x damascena* of Turkey are treated with solvents and water vapor to give essential oil.

The roses are collected and cleaned before being distilled on site by either of these two widely used methods.

The oldest method is the distillation by

Certain roses emit a heady perfume, while others are much more subtle and delicate. The enthusiast in his garden can move from one to the other, beginning with the most mild of scents and ending with the most potent.

water vapor, which allows the harvesting of oily droplets, still called rose essence or essential oil; the condensed vapor becomes rose water. The product not having undergone great heat, it remains fresh, fruity, rosy. This is what enters into the composition of exceptional perfumes.

The distillation by volatile solvents extracts both the vegetable fats and the perfumes, producing a white wax called "concrete." Because it is not entirely soluble in alcohol, it is difficult to use in perfumery. However if melted, it gives one part alcohol solution and one part oily solution, after decanting. This is rose absolute, which emits a much heavier scent than rose essence—a part of the volatile perfume having been lost at

distillation—and gives the most interesting effects in perfumery.

Very small amounts of these products are needed to have a significant effect in perfume preparations. This is a good thing, because rose essence costs $1,500 per pound, while rose absolute fluctuates between $450 and $900. The products may differ slightly depending where they are produced, but their effects are similar in perfumes.

Just as in vineyards, meteorological conditions have an influence on the results: essence and absolute correspond to vintages whose qualities differ by the year. And, again as with wines, it is always possible to improve characteristics in order

Why do roses smell good?

The essential oil obtained from the petals contains nearly 300 molecular constituents, some of which are barely identifiable. This explains why the artificial synthesis of rose fragrance by chemists has not yet been able to imitate nature perfectly.

The perfume is generally concentrated in the glands situated at the surface of the petals and is formed within their cells by a complex alchemy. This is surely one of the reasons why roses with abundant petals are often the most fragrant.

In nature, the scent of small wild roses must have had the attracting of pollinating insects as its only purpose. It then became the time-consuming labor of dedicated rose growers to reinforce this characteristic and to create beautiful fragrant roses.

There is certainly no other flower that can rival the rose in terms of perfume; no other is as rich and varied. While most fragrant flowers have a perfume characteristic of their species, the rose emits an infinite variety of scents that evokes a multitude of other flowers, vegetal elements, plants and fruits.

to obtain fragrances whose qualities are consistent year to year, by blending a bad year with a good one, for example.

Certain very famous perfumes exalt the rose with majesty: Joy by Jean Patou, which dates back to 1935, or the much more recent Paris of Yves Saint Laurent. Even today, Joy stands among the six greatest perfumes in the world, including jasmine and the most beautiful roses of Grasse in its composition.

The pleasure of the perfume maker

If the perfume maker takes pleasure in walking through a rose garden, it is because he loves to test its scent, find new sensual wonders in nature, and imagine still-unknown perfumes. The universe of roses brings him an extraordinarily varied and subtle palette.

The fragrant rose is like a jewel, a precious stone. Along with jasmine, it constitutes the principle base of perfumery: its scent for the perfume maker is luxurious and always new. At its most basic, he will find strange and surprising exhalations: fruity (lemon, raspberry, grapefruit) or aromatic—evoking incense, honey, or even certain resins which can also blend

iridescent nuances, green or powdery. Many roses have a very soft, seductive feminine characteristic reminiscent of cosmetic face powder. There are great nuances in rose perfumes from one variety to another. Some are heady and pervasive, others subtle and elegant.

When he walks among roses, the perfume maker is like an insect, beckoned by different scents, stimulated by a whole spectrum of sensations. In the rose garden, searching for the most sublime inhabitants, he investigates the least spectacular first: they often reveal original scents. Even certain simple old roses that resemble eglantines, or wild roses, have delicious fragrances. He examines the climbing roses: farther from the ground, the flowers have not absorbed its humidity and can unveil other interesting nuances. Then he turns his attention to the larger flowers that more intimately store their perfume. He is trained to classify these sublime flowers into established categories; when he discovers others. he will research their common traits, little by little enriching the accumulated store of learning. A very fragrant rose evokes for the perfumier a pleasurable sensation akin to that stirred by an exceptional perfume. More than all others, the rose is the flower of emotion. How often poets have been inspired to associate it with women and love!

An ever-changing perfume

Fragrant roses elicit praise. Their olfactory richness is fragile and capricious, influenced by sunshine, temperature, humidity, time and length of day…even the soil.

Even the most fragrant roses give their best for only a very short time: patience and perseverance are required to obtain the greatest pleasure from them.

And each person reacts differently too: no two rose lovers will have the same perception of a single rose.

One must take one's time to obtain the full pleasure of a fragrant rose. At each stage, the sensations are different.

In the rain, the rose hides her perfume. The rays of the sun must free the essential oils contained in the petals.

It is not known for certain if a relationship exists between the form and the fragrance of the flower, any more than between its color and its fragrance. Most often, it is the product of chance; the rose so often conceals its perfume under different disguises and reveals it only by surprise. And the strangest scents are sometimes found in flowers whose appearance is nothing less than spectacular. On the other hand, *Rosa gallica centifolia* and *Rosa x damascena* are often used by perfume makers and are very simple flowers. All else aside, the most colorful semi-opened roses generally have the most intense fragrance.

To smell a rose

Don't bring your nose too close to the flower: fresh air must circulate between the petals and your nostrils to tap the sensitive molecular perfume cells.

To smell a rose, be sure to take your time: the first effect—called the "head"—often evokes an unoriginal, very brief fragrance. You must wait in order to perceive the subsequent heavier notes, called the "heart" and the "base." These carry the most significant differences from one perfume to another, while the head note is much more quickly defined:

a citrus fragrance, a scent green or fresh or soft.

The ideal time to enjoy the fragrance of roses is early in the morning, before the flowers have gotten too much sun and are too open. The closed petals form a pocket that traps the scent; once they are struck by the first ultraviolet rays, the buds have energy to open up and free their perfume, which softens as the flower blooms.

The enthusiast in his rose garden takes pleasure in smelling a dozen different varieties throughout the course of the morning, beginning with the softer perfumes and ending with the strongest.

By returning regularly to the most interesting, he will come to discover new olfactory treasures.

This pleasure of a garden of fragrant roses can be prolonged until the very end of day: while the sun weakens and disguises the fragrances, the evening coolness and humidity returns to them their richness. The water molecules with which the atmosphere is recharged will once again transport the scent of the petals to the nostrils of the rose lover.

[The quarrel of the old versus the modern]

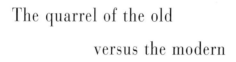

More than the color, it is the variety of shape that has contributed to the success of roses: from the simple five-petaled white or pink eglantine to the colorful globe with nearly a hundred petals, the spectrum is vast.

It was at the beginning of the 1800s that rose growers first popularized the creation of new varieties, selecting hybrids having inherited the best qualities of their parents. These roses of old were generally vigorous shrubs with fragrant flowers of

abundant petals. Old roses continue to have their faithful admirers and this is good: these fans, in the cultivation of their own gardens, contribute to the preservation of this formidable inheritance. There are even associations for enthusiasts of old roses that bring together passionate professionals and amateurs, such as Heritage Roses in North America.

Running counter to this preference is that for the spiraled shape of 20th century roses, which open out from a tightly wound bud. These are the ones usually found at florists as cut flowers. Nevertheless, some choose to follow a "nostalgic" fashion and scorn the most recent creations. That is unfortunate because, more than the date of creation, it is the typical shape of the flowers most devotees of "old" roses seek.

Why do they reproach "modern" roses? They say the bearing of the shrub is rather stiff, the look is not wild enough, the tight spiral bud lacks softness and nuance, the color is too aggressive, and the fragrance is often lacking.

Is the rose sensitive to the effects of fashion? Undoubtedly, and growers at the end of the 20th century understood this well. There are many today who offer older forms, such as the cupped or quartered roses with abundant petals, following the example of the Englishman, David Austin.

Each decade emphasizes different qualities, and the '90s were incontestably those of fragrance. Not only do the most recent creations exhibit the generous forms of old roses with their soft and harmonious colors, they also revive their fragrance. Moreover, they strive for vigorous disease-resistant bushes. So let us appreciate the value of recent advances: by their achievement, the circle is almost complete.

Old roses or modern…there is no quarrel. It has more to do with the notion of shape than of time. Fashion evolves and tastes change, in roses and everything else.

Fragrant roses, décor of your garden

The spectacular effect of roses first delights the sight, with the bearing of the shrubs and the abundance and the color of the flowers.

Fragrant roses truly have a life apart and an appeal to another sensibility. This amply justifies keeping them highly visible—in or near the house, in a seating or high traffic area—to get the maximum benefit. For some varieties, you might want to choose a place out of sight, a small corner of the garden where you can pick them to decorate the house.

The rose has fascinated enthusiasts for centuries. Certainly no other flower is as frequently cited, represented, described, drawn, or photographed.

Dare to blend. The fragrances of roses are not diminished by each other. More likely, a blend of perfumes will provoke entirely new sensations, just as a perfume maker seeks in his quest for perfect beauty.

Do not content yourself to plant the roses in a corner of the garden and leave them to manage on their own, expecting them to enchant you with their color and fragrance. Many roses are happy with little attention—this is the case with wild roses. But even the most sturdy fare better with a little care.

Why is the rose so fascinating?

It is never the same twice: it is beautiful, and different each day, from the appearance of its first bud to the fall of its petals. It changes continually, according to the place it occupies in the garden, the advancing of the season, and the hour of the day. The changes are just as apparent in a cut bouquet. It is not surprising that the rose responds to generous care.

With the exception of the most recent, much more robust hybrids, the most fragrant roses often bloom on medium-sized shrubs with weak or disease-prone vegetation. To be their best, they need a lot of care. Good soil preparation before planting, a sunny and well-ventilated location, mineral enrichment and regular fertilizing, careful watering especially in their early years, and regular pruning and weeding are all routine essentials. Preventive treatment is just as crucial, because their foliage rarely resists attack

On the following pages are evocative displays of the queen of flowers: the portraits of fifty roses chosen from among the most fragrant.

by fungus, and their leaves are often lost long before the usual fall of leaves.

As for climbing roses, which charmingly ascend a wall or arbor, they too demand a measure of care. They must be trained onto their support, since unlike other climbing plants, they have no natural means of clinging to it.

But don't let this discourage you: the few hours dedicated to your roses are a small price for the months of enchantment they will bring you.

For maximum success, you must plant with care, follow a regular maintenance program, and always keep a pair of pruning shears with you when you are walking in the garden to cut the withered flowers, dried branches, and damaged leaves.

Your landscape décor is a matter of taste, of course. Some general principles must nonetheless be observed: roses being greedy shrubs, plant them only near others that are not so demanding. Arrange your plantings so that the eventual growth of one plant will not impinge on another; your roses, in full bloom, should not be hidden behind shrubs or perennials. Consider the relative growth habits and qualities of your chosen plantings; certain low-growing plants will fill in the often bare bases of rose bushes, and perennials with fragrant foliage have a certain repellent power against insects.

In this book, you will find the photos of fifty roses selected from among the most fragrant ever created. Each year, dozens of new roses are offered in catalogs: their availability is often limited and, after only a few editions, they disappear from the pages, replaced by new, more interesting varieties. Others will be lost over the decades.

The ones we have collected here are of very different ages. Many are true old roses, created in the 19th century and some, even earlier. These are the varieties that generations of rose-growers chose to transmit and preserve like a precious heritage. Others are classics of the 20th century whose qualities and fragrances especially, assure them a never-diminished success. And finally, the others are very recent creations that have been made available to amateur gardeners. We have classified these fifty stars by color, which remains the first criterion when an enthusiast wants to define or choose a rose.

The softness of monochrome or more vivid mixes of complements...the blend of colors is, again, a matter of taste. Keep in mind that white lightens the palette and brings out the neighboring colors, blue gives depth, yellow brightens and warms, and red attracts attention and marks the perspectives.

Volume and texture must also be considered: soft flowers, wispy branches or large leaves that contrast well with fleshy roses.

The Reds

"The old flower

Completely new

Wild like oats

Lucid like wheat

One laughs

True as a dream

Beautiful as love

Red as always."

Jacques Prévert—1972—*Choses et autres*

[Strength and sweetness]

Hybridizer: *Garçon*
Year: *1881*
Height: *5 to 7 feet (1.5–2 m) or more*
Group: *Large-flowered bush*

Here is one of the strongest perfumes of all roses: 'Mme. Isaac Pereire' has been a great classic of gardens for more than a hundred years. It bears very large, ruffled deep crimson flowers which one might call unkempt.

At the heart of their fuchsia-red outer leaves touched with carmine, they allow a glimpse of their yellow-brown stamen. The corollas are among the largest, from 4 to 5 inches (10–12 cm) in diameter. The petals turn back on themselves and give a convex look to the flowers, which flatten out in sections, showing precise quarters, and thus forming a perfect rosette. The color of the flower also varies, fuchsia, carmine or magenta, according to temperature and degree of bloom. A great size and perfect shape is most apparent in the flowers of September, those at the beginning of the season often being poorly finished.

However luxurious and proud the large foliage of this superb rose, it is virtually drowned by the flowers, which appear on very short branches.

A large spreading bush

First in June and again in September, this large shrub, which can also be trained as a small climber, is overwhelming in the profusion of its enormous flowers. Vigorous and hardy, adapting well to cold, it is also demanding and, in order to give its best, requires a regular supply of enriching agents and fertilizers, as well as abundant watering during the growing season. On the other hand, it needs only light pruning.

If you grow it as a climber, don't train it too closely so as to avoid diseases, especially rust, to which it is particularly vulnerable: spread it out 4 inches (10 cm) away from a wall with the help of a trellis.

It tolerates semi-shade

'Mme. Isaac Pereire' is a rose with almost limitless possibilities. You can let it grow freely, or train it or support it: it will also happily decorate an arch, small pillar or ramp. It forms lovely garlands, and trains nicely along a horizontal bar to border a lawn. It always prefers to be planted in full sun, but it will tolerate semi-shade. Left free, you can keep it isolated, joining

A true old rose

'Mme. Isaac Pereire' is a true old rose whose origins remain unknown but which is part of the Bourbon family.
These roses get their name from their place of origin, the Ile de la Réunion, called the Isle of Bourbon since 1793. From there they were sent to Paris in 1819, its seeds probably from a rose discovered by chance by the director of the royal gardens of the island.
The first Bourbon roses, which resulted from hybridizations made from this specimen, had bright red semi-double roses of medium size, with large concave petals forming a flat cup.
With a little time and perseverance, the rose growers of the era obtained noticeable improvements from these first varieties.

together three or four stalks, or combine it in a bed with other varieties of roses or even other species. Its color blends very well with yellow flowers.

[Fruity melody]

Hybridizer: *Louis Laperrière*
Year: *1951*
Height: *24 to 32 inches (60–80 cm)*
Group: *Large-flowered bush*

An intense perfume, dominated by red fruits, cassis and raspberries, and deep red petals—a color sometimes called dark crimson—join to form a perfect rose: 'Mme. Louis Laperrière' remains one of the best red roses ever created, embellished with qualities which have been its glory from the time of its introduction.

The forty to fifty petals of this medium size flower overlap very elegantly, and this beauty does not diminish: it does not discolor or turn purple and is not spoiled by the rain. Its flowering begins early in the season and continues with abundance until late. It has a dark matte green foliage.

A thick bush

'Mme. Louis Laperrière' is a very bushy rose, not very large and moderately thorny.

It is solid and plants without a problem, so long as it is assured a short pruning, a supply of compost and fertilizers, and

The charm of the 1950s

'Mme. Louis Laperrière' has the charm of the roses of the '50s. This era saw one of the most beautiful creations of Louis Laperrière, which he named in honor of his wife, and for which he was awarded a gold medal at Bagatelle.

Forty years later, it was a climbing version of 'Mme. Louis Laperrière' which won the Prix de la Ville at the first fragrant rose contest organized in Nantes. This mutation of the bush would be later offered to amateur gardeners.

The Laperrières are a great family of French rose growers: their ancestor Joseph-Martin created the first nursery in 1864. Today, four generations later, Robert, Monique and their son Philippe continue the tradition. From the beginning of the 20th century, there have been approximately 120 new varieties published, and the catalog continues to grow each year with their creations.

sufficient watering. But it is not exempt from diseases and is slightly susceptible to mildew. It is best to treat it preventively several times in the course of the season.

Once they wither, remove the flowers that have not fallen on their own, cutting the stem below the bloom, which brings about the next flowering.

A garden rose

'Mme. Louis Laperrière' is the garden rose *par excellence* for composing beds or borders. Plant three or four stalks—or more—in a triangle to dress up the corner of a sunny lawn.

Its coloring blends effortlessly with other varieties, the beautiful copper yellow of 'Sutter's Gold,' for example. And if you like to blend among species, the choice is plentiful in evergreens and large perennials.

But the classicism of these beautiful flowers provides an exquisite décor all on their own.

You can also cultivate 'Mme. Louis Laperrière' in a large container close to the house where you can better enjoy its fragrance. Don't count on these flowers for bouquets though, as they fade quickly once cut.

[What warmth!]

This magnificent flower, a very recent creation, has all the promise of a long and remarkable career scenting the gardens of fragrant rose lovers everywhere: a powerful and intense scent with a spicy overtone, a perfect shape, and a beautiful deep, very warm red.

The elongated buds spread out, giving noble well-whorled flowers whose forty petals unfurl in a particularly balanced fashion. They are quite large, 4 to 5 inches (10–12 cm) in diameter, and stand out on a very dark green, often matte foliage.

A large bush

'Hacienda' is a large rose bush, which exhibits good vegetation and which, like all the most recent varieties commercialized by their growers for the amateurs, is very disease-resistant. 'Hacienda' is, therefore, an easy rose to grow, demanding only a minimum of care: an annual application of fertilizer, regular pruning, a bit of water if the weather is truly dry.

A touch of amber and spice

'Hacienda' has just begun its career, but is already one of the most award-winning roses of recent years: in 1998 it carried off all the prizes for fragrance in the major international competitions. In 1999, it repeated its "offense," winning the international prize of the City of Nantes. This is a substantial testimonial: the competition that this town organizes every two years submits candidates to a jury composed entirely of professional perfume makers. They noticed in 'Hacienda' "a rosy note at the heart of the floral and marine bouquet, from which escapes a touch of amber and spice in resonance with the sweetness of raspberry."
It was the growers, the Orard family, who chose to name it 'Hacienda,' its beautiful red color and its heady perfume wonderfully evoking the heat of the great plantations at the heart of South American agriculture. Outside France, it is called 'Red 'n' Fragrant,' a name which pretty much sums up its qualities.

Unlike most red roses, 'Hacienda' tolerates all exposures, even the most shady, and its flowers do not suffer as a result.

Without competition

You can combine three to five bushes and form a pretty bed in the middle of a yard, or place 'Hacienda' against a wall and regularly cut its barely bloomed flowers to form highly fragrant bouquets.

But because of its significant growth, it is best to avoid planting it too close to a passageway: neither along a driveway leading to the garage, at the risk of soon needing to buy a smaller car, nor under the windows of the house, where the shutters will quickly become immobile.

Combine 'Hacienda' with other varieties of rose at the risk of diminishing its charm; but the warmth of its flowers is heightened by planting vibrant whites or pale blues nearby. You can also trim its stalks with bushes of soft blue flowers such as lavender or perovskias.

Hybridizer: *Orard (France)*
Year: *1998*
Varietal name: *'Oradal'*
Height: *36 to 44 inches (90–110 cm)*
Group: *Large-flowered bush*

Papa Meilland

[A captivating perfume]

Bush hybridizer:
Meilland (France)
Year: *1963*
Varietal name:
'Meicesar'
Height: *32 to 40*
inches (80–100 cm)
Climbing
hybridizer: *Meil-*
land (France)
Year: *1970*
Varietal name:
'Meisarsa'
Height: *8 to 10 feet*
(2.5 –3 m)

A truly heady and captivating fragrance—referenced as a standard—with rosy and citrusy notes, and a splendid dark red flower: these are the qualities that merit planting 'Papa Meilland' in your garden, even if the rose requires a bit of coddling and its flowering period is short.

For some, this is the most beautiful red flower ever created: the blooms, a deep crimson, are tightly scrolled and give large full double flowers with thirty-five overlapping petals. Their dark velvety red is adorned with reflections of blue-black that become almost black as the flower blooms. Its intense fragrance continues throughout the flowering, regardless of the weather.

These superb roses emerge from a thin but dense bright green foliage.

A rose to coddle

'Papa Meilland' is a bush rose with an erect bearing, which unfortunately is not equal to its very beautiful flowers: it is moderately prolific and very sensitive to mildew and black spot. It requires much care and attention to hold its place in the garden: planting in very rich soil, avoiding too much direct sun (which would burn its petals), regular fertilizing, preventive treatment against disease for the entire season, watering when the weather is dry. But what a pay-off: a bouquet of 'Papa Meilland!'

There is also a climbing version, a mutation of the bush: it has the same prized qualities and the same flaws.

An isolated beauty

It is always preferable to isolate a disease-prone rose in order to avoid transmitting the disease to its neighbors. Combine 'Papa Meilland' with other species of shrub or great clusters of perennials.

But if you want the beautiful effect of mass, you must combine many stalks of this fragile rose. And you will be burdened with the obligation of its maintenance.

In its climbing form, plant this rose on a

Of all his fragrant rose creations, 'Papa Meilland' is Alain Meilland's favorite. And so he baptized it in the early '60s in honor of his grandfather, Antoine, who devoted his entire life to roses, just as did his father, Francis, and many other members of his family.

'Papa Meilland' probably owes its exceptional perfume to a long line of forebears having this same quality. This rose is cultivated not only to perfume gardens, but as a cut rose as well.

'Papa Meilland' was one of the first roses to be patented: like all artists, rose growers have the rights to their creations. In modern French legislation, they receive exclusive financial benefits from their propagation and sale for twenty years before they fall into the public domain. As with many luxury products, roses are often illegally propagated. When such abuses are discovered, rose growers are quick to seize and destroy the counterfeits.

pergola or a lattice fence. In a planting of roses grown for cutting, distance 'Papa Meilland' at least 7 feet (2 m) from the other varieties.

A "red" perfume

A delicious scent of "red rose" emanates from these tightly scrolled double flowers of a beautiful, velvety deep garnet red. They are medium-sized, clustered in bouquets of three to six flowers, and flower repeatedly throughout the summer. They have been known to emblazon the bush even at the end of October and, covered with the morning frost, they continue to exhale their deep perfume.

The deep green foliage is full and magnificent, another pleasure of this variety, which can be grown as a large bush or trained as a climber.

'Red Parfum' inherited all the qualities of greatness: from its "father," 'Souvenir de Claudius Denoyelle,' its color and fragrance, and from its "mother," 'Etendard,' the vigor of its bearing. It reaches 5 to 6 feet (1.5–1.8 m) in height and can even climb to 10 to 13 feet (3–4 m), if given the opportunity; the height it achieves is more a matter of its pruning than of its heredity.

Another of the prized qualities of 'Red Parfum' is its great resistance to disease.

Plant it in fresh soil in semi-shade, especially where the summers are long and dry.

Bush or climbing
If you have enough room to grow free-standing shrubs, plant 'Red Parfum' in groups of three, placed in a triangle and spaced 28 to 32 inches (70–80 cm) apart. By themselves, they are an outstanding display against a lawn's green tapestry. But they combine as well with perennials in similar shades—monardas, lupines, day-lilies.

This very thorny rose will form a rather tall flowering hedge as fragrant as it is defensive. It can also climb a tree, span a fence, or grow against the wall of a house. A northern exposure works well for this variety, whose deep red coloring does best without a great deal of sun. In allowing

Hybridizer: *André Eve (France)*
Year: *1972*
Height: *5 to 6 feet (1.5–1.8 m) as a shrub, 10 to 13 feet (3–4 m) or more for climbers*
Group: *Shrub or climber*

An extra rose

Living in Loiret since the '60s, André Eve is very passionate about old-fashioned roses and he has created a remarkable collection of them, which is open to the public in the high season. He has also set up his own program of hybridization, seeking new varieties that combine the best qualities: bearing, fragrance, and resistance to disease. One of his first creations, and perhaps his greatest success, is 'Red Parfum,' prize-winning since its first year of commercialization in Copenhagen. Its name, conceived to cross borders, conveys its two principal characteristics: its deep velvety red color and its delicious perfume. Its perfect appearance in the garden of its grower is also a criterion of good health, since Eve is known for never using chemical treatments to combat pests.

some branches to hang softly so as to keep the flowers at a good height, you can more easily experience their fragrance.

To promote its continued flowering throughout the summer, remove wilted flowers immediately. To optimize the length of the plant's flowering, keep only the last blooms of the season.

[Scent of a rose]

Bush hybridizer:
Wilhem Kordes
(Germany)
Year: *1935*
Height: *24 to 28*
inches (60–70 cm)
Group: *Large-*
flowered bush
Climbing
hybridizer: *Jackson*
& Perkins (United
States)
Year: *1946*
Height: *13 feet (4 m)*

Very fragrant with the scent typical of a rose are the large double flowers of this famous variety. It is perfectly formed of thirty petals of a beautiful velvety crimson red with hints of purple.

The petals of their tall buds gradually bend back, forming a deep cup and revealing the heart of the flower.

The flowers grow straight at the end of the stems. In a very beautiful effect, stems tend to bend under the flowers' weight, causing them to fall back into the deep green foliage. In summer, 'Crimson Glory' is studded with flowers that reappear intermittently until autumn. But be careful, like many roses of this warm color, they do not like full sun—it burns their petals.

Compact shrub or vigorous climber

The rose bush 'Crimson Glory' remains compact without large growth, but it is full of strength and vigor. It is best given rich soil, regular enriching agents, and a light, rather long pruning (but not in the first two years) to make it fill out. A good application of fertilizer at the end of its first flowering will help assure continued bloom.

Immense fame

This is one of the red roses best known and most widely used by growers in their hybridization work. 'Crimson Glory' is one of the parents, for example, of 'Ena Harkness' and 'Mme. Louis Laperrière,' both of which are included here, and also of many other varieties to which it has endowed, at least in part, its color and its fragrance.

In gardens, this variety has enchanted generations of rose lovers. Even though sixty years has brought a good number of novelties and improvements to rose creations, 'Crimson Glory' remains a standard for its fragrance, and continues to be cultivated and offered in the catalogs of many rose growers.

The abundance and the perfume of these flowers will compensate for their average state of health, which requires regular maintenance. Regular preventive spraying throughout the season gives some reassurance—twice a month, with a rose "anti-disease" spray. A further safeguard is the use of a complete product, reducing the risk of aphids at the same time.

'Crimson Glory' in its climbing form produces a blanket of fragrant roses as well, but repeat flowering of the climber is unusual.

Decorate a tall pillar

'Crimson Glory' is very vigorous in its climbing form and the graceful cascade of its flowered branches has the most beautiful effect. Train it on a large pillar near the house where you will appreciate it most, even before you walk into the garden.

Train the rose to grow along a frame sufficiently distanced from the support to provide good airflow, and attach it throughout with raffia or plastic string tied loosely enough not to risk damaging its branches.

[A delectable scent]

Bush hybridizer:
Albert Norman
Year: *1946*
Height: *32 to 40 inches (80–100 cm)*
Climbing hybridizer: *Murell (England)*
Year: *1954*
Height: *13 to 17 feet (4–5 m)*

A strong, intense, engaging perfume emanates from these very large double flowers. Their pointed, tightly scrolled, deep vibrant red buds open into ample corollas with thirty overlapping reflexed petals. They open to a crimson red, velvety and scarlet, and their shape is especially beautiful. The petals, slightly opened in the center, keep their beauty throughout their entire blooming.

The branches are sometimes not equal to the flowers: grouped in large bouquets, they may make the branches droop under their weight, causing the blossoms to fall back into the dark green glossy foliage. This minor flaw is more pronounced in the climbing version of the rose, giving it a wild and abandoned look.

With good exposure, 'Ena Harkness' can give a particularly early flowering.

A marvel worth noticing

The rose bush 'Ena Harkness' has an erect bearing but is only moderately vigorous. It is therefore important to plant it in rich, regularly fertilized soil. It prefers a warm, sheltered place and tolerates partial shade. Its susceptibility to mildew requires regular attention: a few minutes devoted routinely to preventive treatment is well worth the pleasure of these magnificently fragrant flowers.

As a climber, 'Ena Harkness' is one of the most beautiful climbing red-flowered roses. But it never repeat flowers in the fall.

An impenetrable barrier

'Ena Harkness' is an excellent rose to use for creating a hedge as fragrant as it is functional: its very thorny stems form a practically impenetrable barrier. To make it even thicker, plant a double row, alternating stalks. By cutting back these roses severely in the first year, you will promote new growth at the base in the following years.

The climbing version of 'Ena Harkness'

The famous petals

This rose, even today one of the most famous varieties of red roses, bears the name of the wife of W.E. Harkness, a member of one of the most prestigious families of British rose growers. Robert and Philip Harkness, the sons of Jack Harkness, are the heirs currently running the company and continuing the patient work.

Red and fragrant, and keeping their freshness up to the first signs of wilting, the pleasure of 'Ena Harkness' petals can be prolonged inside the house in many preparations. Dry them and mix them in a potpourri, steep them in oil to scent potpourri, sprinkle them in salad for color, or even crystallize them by dipping them in egg white and then in sugar before drying them in a warm oven.

has a hardy growth; it's a good choice to cover a wall of the house. Allow sufficient distance from the wall to assure good airflow and to avoid attacks of mildew. What a scent when you open the windows!

Guinée

[Nearly black roses]

The large, very fragrant flowers of 'Guinée' are the most beautiful dark crimson red, almost black, and this intense color lasts throughout its flowering.

Even the rounded buds are nearly black. They open in June with large full flowers about 4 inches (10 cm) in diameter, of an extremely deep blood red that appears black in the shade. At the beginning they are slightly cup-shaped, with small irregular petals, some of which bend inward and others out, and have a very soft texture that gives them a scintillating brilliance.

More fully bloomed, the flowers take on an even freer form, with their golden brown stamen coming into view. All the while they retain this remarkable color, so rich against the dark wood and the deep leathery foliage. Just leave them in full sun, which they cannot resist.

A superb climber

'Guinée' is a superb variety, originally a climber. It exhibits strong growth and is capable of covering large surfaces so long as it is guaranteed good soil conditions.

Unfortunately, few rose growers still offer it in their catalogs, perhaps because 'Guinée' is not very hardy.

An evocation of faraway lands

Charles Mallerin, the great rose grower at the beginning of the 20th century, named this rose for Guinea, the small African country that was once a French colony. Being so dark that it seems black in the shadows, naming the flower 'Guinée' undoubtedly evokes that faraway land and its tropical heat.
Few other roses bear the name of a country, except of course, 'La France,' the famous Hybrid Tea rose of Jean-Baptiste Guillot Jr., the ancestor of all our so-called modern roses. Provinces and cities, however, have often lent their names.
Charles Mallerin, whom some consider one of the greatest growers of all time, was not a rose grower by training but, rather, a heating engineer. Hybridization of roses became so strong a passion that he chose it for his career.

Essentially, it requires a very sunny place, but not so sunny as to burn its petals, perhaps covering a warm wall.

From the first frosts, it must be protected by turning the soil around the base and applying a good mulch.

The initial flowering of this rose, already generous, can be prolonged for many weeks: remove the outer floral branches as the blossoms fall off.

Harmony on a pale wall

Given the very deep color of both its foliage and its flowers, 'Guinée' shows particularly well against a light-colored wall. You can soften the contrast with a blue clematis or a climbing rose with white flowers, such as 'Albéric Barbier' or 'Fée des Neiges.'

'Guinée' can also be planted against a trellis to form a tunnel around a bench: it will give the pleasure of its fragrance when you rest there.

Training most of the branches horizontally will encourage the production of more numerous floral buds.

Hybridizer: *Charles Mallerin (France)*
Year: *1938*
Height: *11.5 to 15 feet (3.5–4.5 m)*
Group: *Climbing*

Commandant Cousteau

[When red becomes raspberry]

Hybridizer: *Michel Adam (France)*
Year: *1994*
Varietal Name: *'Adharman'*
Height: *32 to 36 inches (80–90 cm)*
Group: *Large-flowered bush*

Here is a superb red rose with a strong and captivating aroma that sets flowerbeds ablaze. Like many red roses, 'Commandant Cousteau' gives off a fruity fragrance with a raspberry overtone. This top note complements a nuance of classic rose followed, according to specialists, by marine exhalations.

These large flowers of twenty-five petals have a beautiful regular cup shape and balance on a rigid stalk.

The foliage is particularly unusual: plum red turning deep shiny green, with a texture reminiscent of leather.

A beautiful decorative shrub

Even before it is covered with flowers, this decorative shrub draws attention to itself. It's very leafy but not very tall, with a compact and regular bearing. Even when somewhat neglected, it keeps its good shape, showing remarkable resistance to the traditional rose diseases.

'Commandant Cousteau' plants easily and requires only regular upkeep: like all roses with good vegetation, it does not like too severe a pruning, as was once the practice. The plant must always preserve enough wood so that the sap continues to circulate or it can weaken.

Be careful: like many roses of this color, the flowers of 'Commandant Cousteau' risk burning in full sun.

Beautiful splashes of color

To ensure the massive effect of beautiful splashes of color throughout the flowering season (from June to the frosts), plant the stalks in groups of five, seven or a dozen.

Feel free to blend 'Commandant Cousteau' with other species in the composition of your flowerbed or patch: the contrast of its unique foliage is particularly interesting against maritime cineraria.

Its cut flowers do not last long, but their perfume is so strong that, though ephemeral, they will scent the entire room.

The most beautiful rose in France

'Commandant Cousteau' is one of the first creations of the grower Michel Adam, and it has seduced the juries of many competitions: in 1991, it received the title "the most beautiful rose in France" at the international competition for new roses in Lyon, and a week later, the international grand prize at the all-new biannual of fragrant roses in Nantes. And still other medals have been bestowed upon it: Baden-Baden, Rome, Monza. This is undoubtedly one of the most frequently award-winning roses of recent years.

When she was being presented a specimen of this beautiful variety bearing the name of Captain Jacques-Yves Cousteau on a TV show in 1992, British actress Jacqueline Bisset gave homage to that great scholar, describing his flowering namesake as "generous, sound, inscrutable, and piquant…like you. It symbolizes your passion for research. It is a part of nature, which you defend so well."

[A fragrance of queens]

An intense and delicious perfume characteristic of red roses emanates from these large majestic flowers, expressing itself especially in full sun.

These are beautiful perfect double roses, classically overlapping forty to fifty petals whose deep velvety crimson red evolves toward violet as they bloom. The petals then fall on their own, without leaving rosehips at the tops of their stems.

The flowers are sometimes so heavy that their fragile stalks weaken under their weight and hide them in their large satiny foliage.

Stocky bush or climber

As a bush, 'Chrysler Imperial' is of medium vegetation and remains stocky. Its flowering extends over many months, but it is unfortunately very sensitive to mildew and rust. Tend it carefully during its growth period or risk seeing it sadly perish. Keep a close watch over it, and in exchange for the pleasure of its

A great garden classic

This large red rose knew its hour of glory in the mid-20th century and there are still many rose growers today who cultivate and offer this great classic in their catalogs. The flower's deep red color is not found in wild roses. It was this flower's successive hybridizations that created roses modern and old whose shades of red are surely the most numerous and most appreciated by enthusiasts. They are most often the red roses that are fragrant. In the garden, they draw attention and mark perspectives. They are the symbol of passion in the language of flowers, and many myths and legends explain their origin in beautiful love stories.

remarkable fragrance, accept having to treat it regularly to prevent the appearance of disease, especially in heavy soil. Don't forget the basic rules: don't water on the leaves, regularly till the base, and mulch the soil.

'Chrysler Imperial' as a climber has the same large red fragrant flowers and an extended flowering period.

Useful companions

Like all roses especially sensitive to mildew, you should keep 'Chrysler Imperial' relatively isolated from other roses and choose a good, well-aerated spot that has good drainage.

To fill out a border or flowerbed and show it off, combine it with plants that have aromatic foliage such as lavender, absinthe, chamomile, mint or thyme. Their effect may also be beneficial in protecting the roses from parasites and disease. And even if not, the aesthetic effect will not be lost.

The flowers of 'Chrysler Imperial' keep well once cut and contribute to superb bouquets.

Bush hybridizer: *Lammerts*
Year: *1952*
Height: *24 to 36 inches (60–90 cm)*
Climbing hybridizer: *Begonia*
Year: *1957*
Height: *13 feet (4 m)*

Étoile de Hollande

[An exceptional perfume]

Bush hybridizer:
Vershuren (Holland)
Year: *1919*
Height: *20 to 32
inches (50–80 cm)*
**Climbing
hybridizer:** *Leenders
(Holland)*
Year: *1931*
Height: *13 feet (4 m)*

Rich, sublime, and strong is the perfume that emanates from these large, somewhat loose double flowers; they have forty petals of a very beautiful, velvety, and brilliant deep pink that becomes purple as they age.

The buds especially are remarkable: they have an attractive elongated shape and a very dark crimson color.

Once the flowers begin to wither, the petals fall on their own, leaving the shrub tidy.

'Étoile de Hollande' is one of the first roses in the garden to flower. In June, it is remarkable, and it enjoys a second flowering in autumn: in between, it remains in vegetation, very decorative with its plum-colored stems and thick deep foliage.

Bush or climber

As a bush, 'Étoile de Hollande' reveals a very supple bearing, erect and branching, and has a moderate growth rate. It's a good shrub whose only obvious flaw is its susceptibility to mildew, which requires checking it regularly and spraying it with an anti-fungal product several times in the course of the season.

But this rose, which knew a veritable glory between the two wars, is now rare, dethroned by other varieties. 'Étoile de Hollande' is known now more for its climbing version, a mutation obtained twelve years later. Very robust in this other form, the rose also repeat flowers in autumn, but with less fervor.

Dress an old tree

An advantage that 'Étoile de Hollande' as a climber has over its bush form is that, running the length of a wall or over a pergola or an old tree, it offers you its delicious flowers at nose height. The trunk of an old or dead tree is an ideal support for a climbing rose, giving the tree a second life. In planting, distance them at least 2 feet (60 cm) from the trunk and

Hybrid teas

It was in 1867 that Jean-Baptiste Guillot Jr., one of the most famous rose growers of his time, created the first Hybrid Tea, named 'La France,' and characterized by its elongated buds and repeat flowering. Some years later, in 1882, the Englishman, Henry Bennett, who worked along the same lines as Guillot, obtained 'Lady Mary Fitzwilliam.' These two varieties are the origin of all the so-called modern roses.
But why the name "tea?" Very simply, because the first roses imported from China at the beginning of the 19th century sailed over in a boat owned by the Oriental Company of the Indies, chartered primarily for the transport of tea. Crossed with other species by rose growers of the era, they naturally gave birth to "hybrid teas."

place it where it will receive the most light. And since the soil is generally poor at the base of dead or very old trees, provide a good dose of food, and water copiously.

You can also make them climb a wall, distanced from it by at least 4 inches (10 cm) to avoid a confined and humid atmosphere that would be favorable for attacks of mildew.

Marcel Pagnol

[Provençal bouquet]

Hybridizer: *Alain Meilland (France)*
Year: *1995*
Varietal name: *'Meisoyris'*
Height: *36 to 40 inches (90–100 cm)*
Group: *Large-flowered bush*

You can bring all of Provence into your garden by planting this beautiful rose. Its large flowers give off a strong and delicious fragrance of raspberries balanced by hints of rose and citrus.

The large ruby red, nearly black buds are cone-shaped, and as the flower blooms, it opens into a very regular cup of a beautiful velvety red with an average of thirty-six petals. Well overlapped, they reflex, slightly raising the heart of the rose. On the stems, these flowers are solitary or combined in small inflorescenses (clusters) of two, three or four buds, amplifying the warmth of their color and the waves of their perfume.

The foliage of this beautiful shrub is quite dense, dark green and shiny.

A robust plant

'Marcel Pagnol' is an easy shrub to grow, as are most of the recent roses, with a bushy bearing and rather ample vegetation. Though it has a good

The name of the rose

At the moment it's chosen, the name of the rose has great importance for the enthusiast. Growers today know this very well: to pay homage to a little-known person can prove unwise for sales, while the names of celebrities excite enthusiasm apart from all consideration of the shape or color of the flower.

To choose prestigious names is surely worthwhile: Meilland, whose company is in Provence, has given homage to the famous sons of this province by naming some of his recent creations for them. 'Marcel Pagnol' was adopted in 1995 to celebrate the centenary of the birth of the writer and playwright, author of many comedies and films, who died in 1974.

resistance to disease in general, it is slightly prone to mildew.

For the rose to give its best, you must assure it the traditional maintenance and care given to roses: good soil preparation before planting, a supply of enriching agents and fertilizer, ample watering during the first few years, pruning at the end of winter, and spraying twice a week from April to October with a complete product to protect it from attack by disease or aphids.

A scented long-stemmed rose

Like all roses slightly prone to mildew, plant 'Marcel Pagnol' in a sunny and well-aerated location, in clusters or flowerbeds. If you want Provence in your garden, the same grower offers three other varieties that give homage to great writers—'Frédéric Mistral,' 'Alphonse Daudet,' and 'Jean Giono'—you can combine this with them. 'Marcel Pagnol' carries itself well as a rose tree, placing its flowers and their perfume at a good height for sniffing without bending over, while giving depth to your setting. Buy it directly in this form.

It's also a good variety to cultivate for cut flowers, but isolate the shrub you plant for this sufficiently in order to avoid contamination.

Bolchoï

Dramatic fragrance

Hybridizer: *Alain Meilland (France)*
Year: *1996*
Varietal name: *'Meizuzes'*
Height: *28 to 32 inches (70–80 cm)*
Group: *Large-flowered bush*

These large, magnificently contrasted, two-toned flowers of blood and gold have a strong scent of may rose, complemented by more discreet fruity and citrus scents.

Growing one or two on a single stem, they give way to medium-sized cone-shaped buds in the same shades of gold and blood. They have a modern cup shape, combining an average of forty-five vibrant red petals that reflex to display the yellow gold at the center.

The flowers blend well with their dense, thick, almost matte green foliage.

A small well-balanced shrub

The shrub is not very large but it has a strong vegetation and a semi-erect well-balanced bearing. Like all the most recent varieties chosen by the large growers to be commercialized, 'Bolchoï' is only slightly prone to the traditional diseases and requires a regular preventive treatment only about twice a month. If you don't forget the basic maintenance—watering if the weather is dry, especially the first years, feeding in the spring and fertilizing throughout the growing season—its very abundant flowering will continue without interruption until the frosts announcing the beginning of winter.

This is a particularly easy rose to grow that will beautify a place in the garden or on the terrace or balcony.

The charm of the original

In a large garden, create a bed of 'Bolchoï' roses by combining about twenty stalks: with the harmony of its yellow gold and red currant colors, it will form a superb ensemble. If your area is smaller, choose it as a tree: the variety itself is grafted onto a stem of about 40 inches (100 cm) in height. Thus, it forms a veritable rose tree that offers fragrant flowers at the height of your nose over many months. Place it near the house to get the most enjoyment from it.

Slavic appeal

When he began to work with Russian rose horticulturists, Alain Meilland wanted to honor his partners by giving a Slavic name to one of his creations. However there are few Russian words commonly known throughout the world, and even fewer that are appropriate to name a rose. Bolchoï was the name chosen for this red gold rose; it shares the colors of the theater in Moscow, which houses one of the most famous ballet troupes in the world.

In this sumptuous framework the rose was baptized in the spring of 1997, as Moscow duly celebrated its 850 years.

Presented at the international competitions for new roses, 'Bolchoï's' qualities were recognized and rewarded, especially in Rome and Bagatelle.

Being of limited size, 'Bolchoï' is perfect planted in a pot. Select a container at least 16 inches (40 cm) deep with a drainage hole in the bottom.

Nuit d'Orient

[Old-fashioned fragrance]

Hybridizer: *Pat Stephens (New Zealand)*
Year: *1986*
Varietal name: *'Stebigpu'*
Height: *32 to 40 inches (80–100 cm)*
Group: *Large-flowered bush*

Very pleasantly scented, this flower has an entirely unusual shade for this type of modern rose: magenta red turning to purplish-violet with age, as old roses do. The shape of the flowers of 'Nuit d'Orient' moreover, gives them their old appearance, much appreciated by enthusiasts over the years. The very short buds bloom into great cup-shaped flowers, the center petals long remaining turned in upon themselves to hide their stamens. These beautiful roses emerge from an ample foliage, sometimes as solitaires or grouped three or four on a stem. With good exposure and proper care, the rose will repeat flower abundantly over the entire season.

An elevated silhouette

'Nuit d'Orient' ('Big Purple' in North America) is a strong, solid rose bush with an elevated, flared silhouette of medium growth that can reach 40 inches (100 cm) in height. It's about average in terms of maintenance, hardiness, and resistance to the traditional diseases and parasites of roses.

Rose food rich in phosphorous and magnesium is recommended after pruning at the end of winter. It can also be used as a fertilizer throughout its growth, reducing the number of applications. Don't forget regular preventive treatment of this rose, especially when conditions favor the development of diseases—namely, high temperature and humidity.

A beautiful production

A small group of 'Nuit d'Orient' roses will make a superb bed on the edge of a garden or along a path.

The trend over the past several years has been to combine different species. The only risk is a poor combination of colors or too close proximity with other plants as greedy as the rose. But you will always show good taste if you combine red roses with blue-flowered aromatics or perennials, such as columbines or bluebells.

You can also cultivate 'Nuit d'Orient' for cut flowers that hold up well and blissfully scent bouquets.

Red

Although it was offered in only a few catalogs in France, 'Nuit d'Orient' enjoys wide fame and enthusiasts are happy to find it again in nurseries. It is known in North America as 'Big Purple.' Part of the collection of great red fragrant roses that have bloomed profusely in Europe since the beginning of the '30s, it is revitalizing opulence and fragrance. Unfortunately, many of those early flowers faded on the shrub and required exacting care. Today, growers have improved the resistance of these roses a great deal. They stir the imagination by adorning their petals in the most original colors: "never before seen" shades, bright colors, evolving hues. All else aside, whether for the garden or a bouquet, red roses remain most people's preference. And they are often more fragrant than the others.

Double Delight

[A spicy character]

It is certainly not the scent that gives this variety its charm, but rather the original coloring of its two-toned petals—though its spicy notes evoking the scent of citrus fruits have a great deal of character. 'Double Delight's' creamy white petals are trimmed with carmine and grow a deeper red as they bloom. A bed in full sun is a true enchantment, for its view as well as its scent.

When the weather is gray, the colors are less remarkable.

Already cream with a border of red, the urn-shaped buds bloom into medium-sized flowers that overlap their thirty-five petals in a regular and very elegant fashion. Adorning a shiny dark green foliage, the rose flowers continually until the frost.

A good hardy rose

A bit lanky to plant, 'Double Delight' is vigorous and hardy and relatively disease resistant. Watch out, however, for attacks of mildew, which you should guard against

Fragrant bouquets

Juries seduced by the originality of its colors have awarded many medals to 'Double Delight.' And it nicely scents the garden.
It is also particularly interesting for cutting and creating superb bouquets.
Pick the flowers early in the morning or in the cool of evening: in the heat of day, they surrender some of their humidity and will not last long in a vase. Choose half-opened flowers that will open out their petals before your very eyes. Place the entire stem as quickly as possible into a bucket of cool water with cut flower preservative added. Work very quickly, because after a few seconds, the cut end is already closing up and the stem absorbs less water.
Let the flowers rest for a few hours and then arrange your bouquet.

with regular preventive treatment, especially if weather conditions are favorable to its development. Humidity and poor aeration are conducive to this fungus, which eventually dusts the entire shrub with an ugly whitish blanket.

'Double Delight' is a good variety for gardens in more southern climates because it is not sensitive to heat. But frequent rain can rot its buds.

Bush or climbing version

'Double Delight' plants happily in bushes or beds, and you can mix it with another variety of rose or another species altogether.

'Double Delight' also exists as a climber: growers have worked on it to create a mutation that adopts the growth habit of long, trainable branches. The flowers of the climber are just as beautiful and fragrant, and give it the same originality. Unfortunately, its flowering in this form is more limited in duration, not occurring again until almost autumn.

These beautiful fragrant two-toned roses are a wonder in bouquets. Plant a bush in your cutting garden to have them at your disposal regularly without detracting from your flowerbeds.

Bush hybridizer: *H. Swim and A. Ellis (Armstrong Nurseries, United States)*
Year: *1977*
Height: *32 to 40 inches (80–100 cm)*
Climbing hybridizer: *Christensen*
Year: *1985*
Height: *12-15 feet (3.5–4.5 m)*

The Pinks

"*The rose is the most beautiful*
of flowers...
The rose is the fragrance of the gods...
The rose embellishes all things."
Ronsard—ca. 1550—

Ode to Guillaume Aubert

Caprice de Meilland

[Fruity harmony]

'Caprice de Meilland' diffuses spicy nuances of carnation to which is added a fruity note, dominated by blackcurrant, apples and litchis, according to perfume professionals. More simply, its strong perfume has the scent of passion fruit.

The large, classic, very elegant flowers of this rose, approximately 5 inches (12 cm) in diameter, are a luminous Bengal pink, almost red. They are composed of some thirty-five outward-curving, overlapping petals that are nearly white at their base. The small center petals roll inward to form a ball hiding the stamen.

These roses, which appear in small inflorescences of one to five flowers, emerge from a very dense, semi-matte medium green foliage. When they wither, their petals fall on their own, leaving a clean appearance to the shrub.

A vigorous rose

'Caprice de Meilland' belongs to the new generation of hardy rose bushes with a semi-erect bearing and, on the whole, good resistance to disease. On the other hand, they are a bit susceptible to mildew and you must pay attention especially if conditions are not ideal: very high temperature, moderate humidity and insufficient ventilation. Take precautions by spraying preventively with a special formula for rose diseases, or at the first sign of trouble—as soon as you see the young leaves begin to shrivel. Sulfur is also effective, but be sure to use it prudently during strong heat.

A choice place in the garden

The main attraction of 'Caprice de Meilland' is its elegant flowers and captivating perfume. Plant several near the house where you can see and smell them best: on the edge of a flowerbed, around a terrace, or along a path. Light and airy flowering plants nearby will intensify the rich coloring and opulence of these roses.

A fragrant caprice

Don't confuse 'Caprice de Meilland,' a very recent acquisition of Alain Meilland, with the one his father baptized 'Caprice' in the '40s, soon after the end of World War II. The latter was two-toned, pink and yellow—a beautiful blend of colors, certainly—but without much fragrance. At the time, this was not a concern of growers.

This new variety on the contrary, is likely to become a classic for lovers of fragrant roses. In 1997, it received both the prize for fragrance at the international competition of new roses at Bagatelle and the first international grand prize at the fragrant rose biennial in Nantes.

The easiest to cultivate are annuals, but they leave beds empty in winter. Above all, avoid colors that clash: choose white or blue flowers that complement the intense pink of 'Caprice de Meilland.' Stay away from reds and oranges!

Hybridizer: *Alain Meilland (France)*
Year: *1999*
Varietal name: *'Meisionver'*
Height: *40 inches (100 cm)*
Group: *Large-flowered bush*

The McCartney Rose

[A true rose scent]

Here is an unforgettable near-perfect rose: its perfume is strong, intense, and very near the true rose scent, supported by fruity and citrus notes.

The large flowers are very elegant: tightly scrolled buds of a dark Indian pink bloom into large, more lightly colored double corollas with overlapping petals. Those on the outside are thicker and gently bend back to expose the heart of the flower, which keeps its small stamen hidden.

These luminous roses stand out against a foliage that is also very decorative, deep shiny green with a texture somewhat rough.

A rapid growth

This rose has rapid growth and an exceptional vitality, and its thick wood provides it an erect bearing. At the end of winter, prune it rather long to keep its shape and balance and to ensure abundant flowering.

The star of the competitions

Don't be fooled by its English name: this rose is the creation of the French rose grower Alain Meilland, who introduced it in 1992. The former Beatle, Paul McCartney, fell prey to its charm and wanted it to bear his name for the release in Great Britain of his newest album, appropriately titled "Flowers." Alain Meilland considers this one of the most fragrant roses in his collection, which means a great deal. Still the most fragrant, according to his preference, is 'Papa Meilland.' That the 'McCartney Rose' is a stunning success is also the opinion of specialists. This variety is the most awarded in the history of Meilland: no less than twenty-two medals in competitions for new roses since its premiere in 1988. It has garnered many gold medals in the prestigious competitions at Monza, Geneva, Le Roeulx, and The Hague, as well as the fragrance prize at Bagatelle. A true star of the garden!

Hybridizer: *Alain Meilland (France)*
Year: *1988*
Varietal name: *'Meizeli'*
Height: *40 to 44 inches (100–110 cm)*
Group: *Large-flowered bush*

The 'McCartney Rose' is not fussy and will tolerate poor soil, if need be. It is indifferent to cold and heat, and is resistant to disease, especially black spot. In fact, this rose is wonderfully easy to grow.

A place of choice

Three or five roses planted in a staggered arrangement will form a beautiful bed on a carpet of grass. But you can also combine the 'McCartney Rose' with other plants in a flowerbed, interspersing good-sized shrubs between each stalk. Its very sophisticated flower is enhanced by neighboring clusters of blue: why not a buddleia, for example, whose arching branches will rest gracefully on the roses. The base of the shrub is nicely decorated with a groundcover of nepetas.

If you have a corner of your garden reserved for roses to cut throughout the summer, the 'McCartney Rose' will be welcome there, since its perfume is unforgettable.

Rose à Parfum de L'Haÿ

[A rose nursery perfume]

A wonderful spicy aroma emanates from these large double flowers formed of small, pretty cherry red petals with lilac casts. They are arranged in robust corollas that gently bend in bouquets at the tops of their stems. This rose constantly repeat-flowers on a bushy and thorny shrub, with smooth but very veiny leaves of a deep matte green.

It was the hope of its grower, Jules Gravereaux, at the beginning of the 20th century, to replace the famous old-fashioned Damask rose with this one. The older rose was grown for centuries for its fragrant petals and is, in fact, one of the grandparents of the 'Rose à Parfum de L'Haÿ'. It had even more fragrance and repeat-flowering. But the 'Rose à Parfum de L'Haÿ' remains a rose for the gardens of enthusiasts and has never been adopted by cultivators.

A thorny and flowering shrub

The 'Rose à Parfum de L'Haÿ' is a vigorous shrub, a hybrid of *Rosa rugosa*, with extremely fragrant flowers.

Unfortunately, it is prone to all types of disease, especially rust and mildew. Every precaution should therefore be taken to ward off attacks: an isolated and well-aerated location, and especially, systematic preventive treatments throughout the season, ending with a treatment with mineral oil in the winter.

The "dog-days" of summer in more southern climates can contribute to chlorosis in plants growing in chalky (alkaline) soil: the 'Rose à Parfum de L'Haÿ' prefers a rich fresh soil and partial shade for some of the day. It will blossom much better with careful tending.

A large isolated rose

Despite its susceptibility to disease, the 'Rose à Parfum de L'Haÿ' with its very pretty flowers and interesting scent may

be perfect in your garden. Keep this large rose isolated in clusters, or combine a few stalks if the space available is larger.

If you keep the final wilting flowers, you will ensure a colorful display in winter of the rose's fruit.

It is also possible to cultivate this rose in a large container: choose one in terra cotta whose warm coloring will blend with that of the flowers, and fill it with good compost for roses.

Hybridizer: *Jules Gravereaux (France)*
Year: *1901*
Height: *48 to 60 inches (120–150 cm)*
Group: *Large-flowered bush*

The first rose nursery

'Rose à Parfum de L'Haÿ' is one of the acquisitions of Jules Gravereaux, the "father" of the rose nursery, which was the glory of the little community of Val-de-Marne.

In 1892, Jules Gravereaux, then the right arm of Aristide Boucicaut, founder of the enormously successful French chain of stores called Bon Marché, decided to dedicate himself to his passion for roses. He acquired a piece of land at L'Haÿ and, little by little, through discoveries, purchases, and exchanges throughout the world, amassed an impressive collection. By the end of five years, he had collected nearly 1,500 varieties. To showcase them better, he contacted his friend Édouard André, who was a landscape gardener. André created for him the first rose nursery in history. In 1910, the collection of over 7,000 shrubs was the only one in existence. But Jules Gravereaux was not content simply to admire them: he cataloged his roses, creating a miniature descriptive card for each one, and he also tried hybridizing to develop new ones. The 'Rose à Parfum de L'Haÿ' is one of these.

[The allure of old roses]

Hybridizer: *David Austin (Great Britain)*
Year: *1986*
Varietal name: *'Ausbord'*
Height: *48 to 60 inches (120–150 cm)*
Group: *Large-flowered bush*

An intense, captivating perfume typical of old roses emanates from these very heavy, very double flowers with large rounded petals whose vibrant warm pink darkens toward the center. This pink turns almost red when the weather is cool.

The large flowers are flat when they first emerge from their buds, but then the wavy petals open in a spiral that gives them a puffy look.

The foliage is generous, dark matte green, with pointed leaflets. It resembles the Portland roses, which is not surprising since 'Gertrud Jekyll' is a hybrid of another "English Rose" by David Austin and the old rose 'Comte de Chambord.'

An erect shrub

'Gertrud Jekyll' is a vigorous and slim shrub, sometimes a bit unbalanced with its long branches. A long pruning is essential to give it a more compact look, based on the golden rule: long pruning for a vigorous rose, short pruning for a weaker one.

If you want to prolong its flowering and be charmed once again by its roses in autumn, plant 'Gertrud Jekyll' in fertile land and feed it well through the summer. It also requires a great deal of watering, followed by a good hoeing that will help retain the necessary humidity. Regular preventive treatment will also protect it against bad attacks of fungus.

A pretty base for a bed

Because this is a rather large rose, several stalks of 'Gertrud Jekyll' may serve as a base for a bed in a sunny spot, but make sure they remain accessible. Don't forget that if you prune them too little, cutting only the old wood, the successive flowerings will be reduced.

'Gertrud Jekyll' goes well with old-fashioned roses and blends with all types of plants. Avoid placing it too close to invasive species, however. It can also be cultivated as a small climbing vine.

Homage

David Austin baptized this rose in honor of the great English landscaper, Gertrud Jekyll, who lived in the 20th century, and was trained as an artist. But as she grew increasingly myopic, she focused more on gardens, and wrote a number of books sharing her concepts for their design. Impassioned by the style of "parish gardens," she admired vibrant colors and carefully considered the shapes and silhouettes of plants in designing colorful flowerbeds whose charm evolved throughout the seasons. Working with architects, she learned how to arrange the plants in a natural fashion within a rigid structure. Gertrud Jekyll designed nearly four hundred gardens, and her ideas still have force a hundred years later. The rose that bears her name is the first to have been selected in England in two hundred fifty years to produce rose essence.

Comte de Chambord

[Simply classic]

All the charm of old roses, with the heady perfume typical of Damask roses, is evident in these flowers. They have a very compact cup shape, with petals in quarters folding towards the center, and a pretty pink color, deeper at the heart, with shades of lilac mauve.

These flowers are truly beautiful at all stages of their blooming, from the buds surrounded by a leafy finery with very high and very pointy sepals, to their fading, when the petals spread on the ground without spoiling the stems.

These flowers balance on supple branches, enveloped by an ample deep green—almost gray-green—foliage.

Hybridizer: *Moreau-Robert*
Year: *1860*
Height: *40 to 60 inches (100–120 cm)*
Group: *Large-flowered bush*

A full sun rose

'Comte de Chambord,' a beautiful, erect and vigorous shrub, grows to approximately 40 inches (100 cm) in height.

Although it is not very prone to disease, it requires the best growth conditions and attentive care: a good pruning in spring is worthwhile prevention against disease. This is a full sun rose which detests shade. It repeat-flowers very well—unlike 'Jacques Cartier,' the old rose it greatly resembles—and it will be even more generous if placed in the best soil and sun conditions.

A decorative rose

'Comte de Chambord' is an extraordinary old rose that can find a place in even the smallest gardens. It can even be grown in a pot.

Because it does not have a very large growth, you can plant several stalks in a small bed under your windows to savor its strong, almost heady perfume.

It blends nicely with other old roses in different shades of pink, such as 'Jacques Cartier,' which has practically the same growth habit. Its beautiful color also blends very well with light blue flowering shrubs.

The cut flowers of 'Comte de Chambord' hold up well and you can make sumptuous bouquets of true old roses with them.

A true old rose

'Comte de Chambord' is a hybrid Portland rose. These roses were the first to benefit from the genetic makeup of Rosa chinensis when they were introduced into Europe from China at the beginning of the 19th century. One of their desireable qualities is their prolonged flowering over the entire summer: for gardeners of the era, this "reflowering" was a veritable revolution.

At the time, the names of roses were not registered as they are now. And it so happened that several professionals gave different names to the same variety. As a result, there was much confusion and many errors. Thus, this same rose is also frequently called 'Mme. Boll.' In fact, the name 'Comte de Chambord' was an honor given in 1860 by its growers, Moreau and Robert, to the candidate for the throne of France.

Aloha

Velvety scent

Hybridizer: *S.E. Boerner & Perkins (United States)*
Year: *1949*
Height: *10 feet (3 m)*
Group: *Large bush or small climber*

These pink roses, whose petals have darker reverse sides tinged with salmon, are very fragrant. They form very full rosettes with sixty overlapping, winding petals, exact copies of the old roses that they call to mind. These beautiful flowers are not afraid of rain or sun. The abundant spring flowering is interrupted in the middle of the summer and begins again in autumn with even more effect.

The foliage is full, shiny and tough.

This is the most fragrant of the pink climbing roses.

A vigorous rose that asks only to climb

'Aloha' is a moderately vigorous rose with erect vegetation that can be pruned as a shrub or trained as a small climber.

As a shrub, it forms a very lanky plant, whose arched branches fall under the weight of a profusion of flowers. You must form it in its first years of planting, and

An American rose

Some time after World War II, the American grower S.E. Boerner was one of the first to recreate through hybridization a rose in the style of the old roses: abundant petals, a changing perfume and color, and a substantial repeat-flowering (a continued flowering over many months, from June to October). He created a precursor to the type of rose that enthusiasts still appreciate today, not necessarily a true old rose but a recent creation with an old-rose look. The British grower, David Austin, creator of the famous 'English Roses,' used this variety a great deal in his hybridization work.

then in March cut back the branches by one-third of their length. If you prefer to train it as a climber, plant it along a fence or pillar, which it will cover in a few years. In this case, do not prune the first few years—allow it to grow as it wants.

'Aloha' is a relatively easy rose to grow, so long as you look after its planting and maintain it regularly. It adapts to cold and is not very susceptible to the traditional diseases of roses.

A scented covering

'Aloha' is a superb rose that will enhance a garden with its fragrant flowering lasting many months, uninterrupted by the heat of summer.

In a small garden, plant three stalks in a triangle, spaced 20 inches (50 cm) apart, choosing a location with good sun exposure.

The warm color of these roses blends easily with other flowers. Mix it fearlessly with perennials or annuals.

You can train it along a wall near the entrance or a window of the house that opens onto its perfume. You will also be guaranteed a beautiful effect by planting 'Aloha' at the top of a low retaining wall and letting it cascade down.

The very long stems of the flowers make for beautiful bouquets.

[A touch of citrus]

A strong perfume whose top note is spicy, enhanced by waves of rose and citrus, accompanies these large, classically beautiful double flowers. Slightly pointed, with forty heavily overlapping petals, they are almost two-toned: the deep pink of the petals, which specialists call 'Solferino purple,' is softened on their undersides. Its flowering extends over many months. But be careful of the exposure you give these roses: their beautiful coloring burns in heavy, direct sun.

Compact bush or climber

'Baronne Edmond de Rothschild' is a vigorous variety with pretty, dense, deep green foliage, the solid stems of which are very thorny. This bush, which remains compact, does not exceed 40 inches (100 cm) in height, and will withstand extreme weather conditions, be it extreme cold or heat. It is relatively disease resistant; nonetheless treat it preventively with a special mixture during the growing period.

The Baronesses

Don't confuse this rose, created at the end of the '60s by the French rose grower Alain Meilland and dedicated to the Baroness Edmond de Rothschild, with 'Baronne Adolphe de Rothschild.' The latter is another very fragrant, superb pink old rose, dedicated by its grower, Pernet Père, to one of her ancestors, as the name indicates.

The parents of 'Baronne Edmond de Rothschild' were themselves two of Meilland's stars, 'Baccara,' (which won its fame as a cut flower—one of the rare varieties of cut flowers whose name you probably know) and 'Mme. Antoine Meilland,' better known throughout the world under the name 'Peace,' which it was given at the end of World War II. It is, even today, one of the most frequently purchased roses in the world.

'Baronne Edmond de Rothschild' also comes as a climber, the result of a mutation. Equally healthy and vigorous, in spring and autumn it is abundantly adorned with beautiful and fragrant flowers.

A choice spot near the house

The superb deep pink coloring and perfect shape of these very classic flowers call for this rose to be planted in beds of a single variety in groups of five to seven stalks.

In a flowerbed, highlight its qualities by blending it with very different species: somewhat relaxed-looking shrubs or blue-colored perennials whose softness will ease the stiffness of its stems.

But 'Baronne Edmond de Rothschild' can bring you even greater pleasure as a climber: plant it near the house, letting it climb a pergola or wall, so long as it is not in full sun. This provides all the more enjoyment of its strong perfume.

Bush hybridizer: *Meilland (France)*
Year: *1968*
Varietal name: *'Meigriso'*
Height: *36 to 40 inches (90–100 cm)*
Climbing hybridizer: *Meilland (France)*
Year: *1974*
Varietal name: *'Meigrisosar'*
Height: *10 to 14 feet (3–4 m)*

Mme Caroline Testout

[So delightful, so fragrant!]

These large, satiny, intense pink ruffled flowers are reminiscent of cabbages. They are deliciously perfumed like old roses and emerge from very pointed buds to stand straight on firm stems. The heart-shaped petals curl outward and crumple at their edges, and the elevated center of the corolla gives the flowers a globular appearance which they keep until they fade, without ever opening entirely.

These beautiful roses, repeat-flowering in bouquets throughout the summer, bloom even in poor weather and are spoiled only by too heavy rains. The satiny green foliage with rounded leaflets is soft to the touch.

A vigorous old lady

'Mme. Caroline Testout' is a perfect example of a Hybrid Tea, those roses with large beautiful flowers appreciated for their hardiness and the length of their flowering. This is one of the oldest varieties of this family still to be offered by rose growers.

A splendid career

Pernet-Ducher, the grower of this old variety, is the heir of two great rose growing families who rivaled in skill at the end of the last century: the Pernets and the Duchers. As the story goes, he was preparing to destroy the seedling of this rose, which he thought mediocre, when the designer Caroline Testout offered to buy it from him and make it the symbol of her company.

'Mme. Caroline Testout' retains its fame even today and still seduces lovers of beautiful fragrant roses. The French Post Office has honored it by selecting it, along with two other famous old roses, 'La France' and 'Mme. Alfred Carrière,' to illustrate a block of three stamps. They were issued in May of 1999 to celebrate the world congress of old roses held that month in Lyon.

This acquisition of Pernet-Ducher is a bush of medium size, but the climbing mutation discovered by Chauvry ten years later is a sumptuous vigorous rose. Each of them, well planted and maintained, will have a remarkable longevity and will grace your garden for many, many years.

They demand close attention in pruning, feeding, and treatment against disease, but will tolerate limited poor conditions, such as partial shade.

To train the climber's branches—since they are often stiff—encourage them to bend while they are still young and flexible.

A superb climber

The bush 'Mme. Caroline Testout' is still available, but you will more easily find the climber, which romantically cascades its beautiful heavy flowers. This rose of exceptional vigor and flowering merits a special place: it draws attention trained on a wall that it will cover all summer long with pretty, well-proportioned flowers. Its soft, sweet perfume is an enchantment when one draws near.

In the garden, you can also appreciate the way it climbs up a pillar or small arch.

If you like blending different species, the pink color of 'Mme. Caroline Testout' works charmingly with the blue flowers of clematis.

Bush hybridizer: *Pernet-Ducher (France)*
Year: *1890*
Height: *24 to 36 inches (60–90 cm)*
Climbing hybridizer: *Chauvry (France)*
Year: *1901*
Height: *15 feet (4.5 m)*

Compassion

[Opulent and suave]

Hybridizer: *Harkness (Great Britain)*
Year: *1973*
Height: *10 to 13 feet (3–4 m)*
Group: *Climbing*

'Compassion' is a superb climbing rose whose deep blue-toned, abundant foliage is ornamented for many months with subtly shaded salmon-colored flowers with hints of apricot orange.

These flowers, like those of classic Hybrid Teas, are perfectly shaped, large and opulent, often grouped several on a stem. They unveil their stamens as they bloom, exhaling suave and soft scents.

A superb climber

'Compassion' has somewhat rigid branches, which are not always easy to train, but it climbs vigorously on its support, forming a plant beautiful for both the elegance of its flowers and its vegetation.

As with many varieties of the latter 20th century, one criterion for selection was the duration of flowering, which can be many months.

This is also an excellent plant for resistance to the traditional diseases of roses. Planted in good conditions and sufficiently aerated, 'Compassion' thrives and your "medical" interventions remain fairly infrequent.

A fragrant hedge

Modern, average-sized climbing roses such as 'Compassion' are perfect for blanketing a retaining wall or low fence. You can also train it on a trellis to scent the passage to your outdoor dining room.

Many species of plants work well with climbing roses: clematises, which climb, similar to roses, or blue delphiniums, bellflowers or irises around their base. Let your imagination go, just avoid those colors that are too close and might clash. But don't be afraid to experiment: a failure is easily redone the following year.

If you have enough room, you can let 'Compassion' develop as a large, somewhat wild shrub in the middle of a lawn, or even use it as a decorative hedge along a wall or to line a row of conifers.

Compassion

Such is the pretty English name under which you will admire this relatively new rose in North America. Be it 'Belle de Londres' (in France) or 'Compassion,' it is considered one of the best modern climbing roses, adding the fragrance of its flowers to its other valued qualities. In only its first few years, it has already received many awards at international competitions for new roses, such as the Royal National Rose Society Edland Medal for Fragrance. This rose is a recipient of the famous ADRN (All Deutsche Rosen Neuheitenprüfung), a distinction awarded by the Germans for the most interesting roses, after very strict tests for resistance.

Albertine

[Fruity trail]

A penetrating and fruity aroma appreciable from far away embellishes the full double flowers of this climbing rose. The large, pointed, vibrant salmon pink buds bloom into flowers whose interior petals are a coppery buff color, while their exteriors change from salmon to coppery pink. They lighten with age to become a pale pink. The ruffled petals have an irregular contour and give the flowers a beautiful, relaxed, crumpled look, almost snow-covered.

The long, abundant flowering period illuminates a dense foliage of small, rounded, deep shiny-green leaflets.

In the spring, this very thorny rose displays coppery red stems that blend well with the shade of the young leaves.

It loves the sun

'Albertine' appreciates sun and heat, and its flowering is early. It is at home in more southern climates, but it will acclimatize successfully in diverse climates and soils.

A very popular climber

In the heat of summer evenings, it perfumes the entire garden. And in addition to sight and scent, 'Albertine' gives sound: birds seem to love it. This is a true old rose in the tradition of its forebears that have seduced generations of gardeners. It can still be found on rusted old arches and crumbling walls, having been planted fifty-some years ago.

Its creator, a Frenchman named Barbier, developed a series of vigorous climbing roses at the beginning of the 20th century, improving them through cross breeding with a rose brought from China in 1860 named Rosa wichuraiana. *'Albertine' is the most popular of this series, but 'Albéric Barbier,' 'Alexandre Girault' and 'Auguste Gervais' also continue to scent many gardens.*

This climbing rose requires impeccable planting and care for good growth, with a good supply of enriching agents and fertilizer and a minimum of maintenance: a tidy-up pruning after flowering and a preventive treatment against disease. 'Albertine' is somewhat prone to mildew. But the risk is limited if you place it at a good distance from the wall on which you train it, with a trellis in between or, better, if you plant it on an open fence.

Remove wilted flowers—they keep their petals, which quickly become unsightly. If you don't have the time to cut them one by one, remove the whole bouquet by cutting the stem at the second or third leaf. As a result, the rose looks clean, and it is freed to concentrate its energy on forming new shoots and buds. But limit pruning to the very minimum: you will thus create a true cascade of flowers.

A classic of gardens

Despite its few drawbacks, 'Albertine' is an exceptional variety, one of the most widely used roses. This climbing rose adapts perfectly to all situations.

Its salmon pink coloring blends especially well with warm stone and brick colors—ochre, sand, gold—any material whose color has a yellow base. It's also an interesting subject for decorating a low wall, an open-weave fence, or a wooden fence, where its branches will cascade to the ground. A pleasing effect is also assured when it's planted against a dead tree or a pylon.

'Albertine' can stand alone in all its splendor, but it mixes nicely too with other plants, such as peonies, or such climbers as clematis and wisteria, which will grow together with it.

Hybridizer: *Barbier (France)*
Year: *1921*
Height: *13 to 20 feet (4–6 m)*
Group: *Climber*

Sonia Rykiel

[A great classic]

Hybridizer: *Guillot/Massad (France)*
Year: *1995*
Varietal name: *'Masdogui'*
Height: *4 feet (120 cm)*
Group: *Large-*

The fruity perfume of this flower matches the elegance of its shape: a large silky cup with a good hundred ruffled petals, in quarters, of a tender pink with hints of amber.

It is quite large, reaching 5 inches (12 cm) in diameter. This gossamer crinoline, balancing on a tender green stem, emerges from a small triangular deep-pink bud. Curiously, this very modern-shaped bud gives birth to a flower whose look is typical of an old rose. These flowers and their buds, which repeat-flower ceaselessly throughout the season, nestle elegantly in the heart of a soft matte green foliage.

A robust and supple shrub

'Sonia Rykiel' has a very supple bearing, which gives it great softness without taking away from its solidity and robustness.

It is very healthy, and not prone to the traditional diseases of mildew or black spot. Preventive treatment is not needed. Aphids are the only reason to use any sort of spray.

After a short pruning at the planting, long pruning is recommended to encourage maximum flowering for this vigorous shrub. Supply enriching agents and organic fertilizer, as well as thorough watering during prolonged dry spells.

A superb bed

The effect of three or five 'Sonia Rykiel' roses planted in a bed is superb. Simply space them 40 inches (100 cm) apart to allow these vigorous shrubs the potential to develop fully.

Some shorter flowering shrubs planted close by will particularly showcase them.

A beautiful aesthetic effect is also guaranteed if you blend them with blue-toned perennials.

These magnificent flowers with the look of old roses are wonderful in bouquets and they hold up well when cut. The 'Sonia Rykiel' rose is a good easy-to-grow subject in a spot reserved for cut flowers.

High fashion

A renowned specialist and collector of old roses, representing a family of rose growers for no fewer than five generations, Jean-Pierre Guillot is also a grower.

Among his most recent creations, prepared in collaboration with his cousin, Dominique Massad, 'Sonia Rykiel' is his favorite. When he proposed to name it in honor of talented fashion designer Sonia Rykiel, she accepted enthusiastically, happy to give her name to this superb flower.

This rose belongs to a new family characteristic of Guillot's style, the Générosa roses; it blends the abundance of the old roses with the modern varieties' diversity of colors. Like all growers at the end of the 20th century, Jean-Pierre Guillot was aware of the changing demands of gardeners, so many of them choosing the forms and fragrances reminiscent of old roses.

Martin des Senteurs

[A perfume that scoffs at rain]

Hybridizer: *Michel Adam (France)*
Year: *1998*
Varietal name: *'Adabaluc'*
Height: *32 to 40 inches (80–100 cm)*
Group: *Clustered-flower bush*

The French name of this very new variety refers to its most remarkable quality: a voluptuous and intense perfume—present even in rain and drizzle—reminiscent of certain exotic fruits blended with a soft citrus note. (*Senteur* is a form of the French verb meaning "to sense or smell.")

These large bouquets comprise twenty to thirty beautiful, buff-apricot, slightly pink buds, which bloom into medium-sized flowers 3 inches (8 cm) in diameter. When full-bloomed, their thirty-six petals have a coloring slightly lighter than that of the buds.

The splendid dark green foliage is marbled with purple, becoming solid colored and glossy as it ages.

Even in winter, having lost its leaves, 'Martin des Senteurs' has a beautiful appearance, its high quality wood remaining attractive.

Sure and carefree

'Martin des Senteurs' is an erect, somewhat smaller rose, a bit rounded at the top. It's one of the new generation of shrubs which not only enchant us with their flowers, but have a good constitution, not being easy prey to disease.

This doesn't mean it can grow all by itself. Like all good roses, 'Martin des Senteurs' appreciates a neatly kept ground, a fairly long pruning in February, an application of Bordeaux mixture after each pruning, weekly watering, and regular feeding and treatment against disease, choosing from the wide variety of chemical and organic formulas, according to your philosophy.

Ideal for small gardens

If you have a small garden, don't hesitate to plant 'Martin des Senteurs' there: when the air warms up in the afternoon, it will scent the entire place. It produces a nice effect alone in clusters of three or five stalks, or in a flowerbed mixed with other species.

It also makes splendid bouquets: a few branches will perfume the entire room.

The Garden of Fragrances

This rose was baptized in honor of the mayor of a small town on the Côte d'Armor named Louis Martin. He was so enamored of this flower that he dedicated a new municipal garden to it, poetically named "Le Courtil des Senteurs" ["The Garden of Fragrances"], after having created an association for rose lovers. And he communicated his passion to all his townsfolk: the gardener in charge of his 500 varieties of roses came to hybridize them, and each new rose born of these chance cross-breedings is offered to a newborn child of the village, and is named after that child.
Michel Adam, the hybridizer of 'Fragrant Martin,' lives in Brittany. He works to combine the beauty and hardiness of shrubs with powerfully fragrant flowers. This variety has won two medals in rose competitions, in Baden-Baden in 1997 and in Madrid in 1999.

But be forewarned: don't plant this rose where you will be annoyed by insects gathering nectar. According to the report of an American journalist who studied several varieties, 'Martin des Senteurs' is a favorite of bees.

Verdant harmony

Hybridizer: *Alain Meilland (France)*
Year: *1995*
Varietal name: *'Meitebros'*
Height: *36 to 40 inches (90–100 cm)*
Group: *Large-flowered bush*

Here is a superb and rather exceptional perfume: a citrusy top note, and fruity and rosy hints that last a long, long time….

The flower of 'Frédéric Mistral' is light pink—some call it Venetian pink—and very well formed, with overlapping petals whose edges gracefully bend back. It is a rose of perfect classicism. The flowering of this rose, a very recent acquisition, is abundant and uninterrupted over the span of many months. It grows on a very pretty, dense, and medium green semi-matte foliage.

A particularly hardy rose

'Frédéric Mistral' is among the most hardy in the Meilland collection. It has good growth, reaching 40 inches (100 cm) in height, and good resistance to disease. It will tolerate some neglect. But like all roses, it reveals its truest splendor only if you spend a bit of time on it: feed it after pruning and after the first appearance of flowers to guarantee the most beautiful and longest flowering. Watering is needed if the weather is very dry, especially the first few years, and always avoid wetting the foliage. Annual pruning is important for the balanced growth of the shrub.

Superb cut flowers

If this rose seduces you particularly by its color and you love its classic form, plant a whole group of them—ten, fifteen or even twenty stalks. For many months they'll be an enchanting sight…and scent!

This rose is ideal for cutting, but avoid picking its long stems after July 31st—this will curtail its repeat-flowering. Be sure to remove the wilted flowers right above the next bud below it.

'Frédéric Mistral' mixes well with other species, particularly light blue or violet perennials and annuals: cosmos, fennel, gypsophilia.

Provence in flowers and poetry

Wanting to pay homage to his adopted land, Alain Meilland gave many of his roses the names of great Provençal writers. Frédéric Mistral was one of them, celebrating this flower in his "Poème du Rhône," ("Poem of the Rhône"— "Lou Pouèmo dou Rose" in Provençal, the language in which he wrote): "Gold, parasol-shaped, perched at the tip of a rush, the pink flower blooms alone in the vase with a small drop, not great. –But Drac, Anglore said, why do you love this flower so much? –I like it, he responded, because it reminds me of you... Aren't you the flower of love, you, who, born like it in the womb of water, symbolize the unique and primitive tenderness of a world which is new and shining with youth!" In international competitions, 'Frédéric Mistral' has won many prizes for the excellence of its perfume.

Conrad Ferdinand Meyer

[Fragrance of nostalgia]

Hybridizer: *Hermann Müller*
Year: *1899*
Height: *up to 10 feet (3 m)*
Group: *Large-flowered bush or small climber*

There is a strong fragrance of old roses in these very full, cup-shaped double flowers, about 5 inches (12 cm) in diameter. They are borne on vigorous, very straight stems spiked with thorns. Their soft pink is adorned with silver highlights, and as they age, the petals reveal a yellow heart. The flowers trim a light green foliage with thick round leaflets. A rare trait in turn-of-the-century roses: it flowers again in September.

It defies the passing of time

This is a climbing shrub whose hardiness comes, in part, from its ancestor *Rosa rugosa*: it resists intense cold and inclement environmental conditions like wind, salt, and air pollution. Robust and vigorous, its stiff stems come armed with large red-brown thorns.

Its dimensions will depend on your decision to prune: whether you regularly cut it back to create a beautiful bush or allow it to form a small climber. It can climb up to 10 feet (3 m).

The doctor's long-surviving patient

This great rose is all that remains of a German country doctor's passion. Hermann Müller, captivated by roses, hybridized them after his retirement. As a friend of Jules Gravereaux, the creator of the Haÿ-les-Roses nursery at Val-de-Marne, he was certainly well schooled. He focused on the search for his ideal: hardy roses that were resistant to frost and had abundant, fragrant flowers. Hermann Müller earned a great number of prizes for his work. He even refused a medal once: a bronze in 1891, because he felt insulted by third prize.
His 'Conrad Ferdinand Meyer,' commercialized in 1899, remains an exceptional rose today, one of the most well-known and cultivated hybrids of Rosa rugosa. *It was baptized in honor of the Swiss German-language poet and novelist who died the year before.*

Dress up the base

Pruned at least in the first few years, it will form a nicely dense and bushy shrub. It's delightful in combination with other varieties of roses that are more leafy at their base, and with other low-growing plants. Lavender, perovskias, and blue-flowered perennials, for example, will embellish the bases of the stems; these can look a little bare, since they grow up 40 inches (100 cm) from the ground before they start to branch.

'Conrad Ferdinand Meyer' appreciates a rich, well-fertilized soil. It doesn't like very dry summers and will call for regular watering in this situation. It also demonstrates some sensitivity to rust and mildew, against which you must guard with regular treatment.

The faded flowers don't fall, so remove them by hand. Though in bloom they are transcendent, they are something less as shriveled-up balls. Sadly, this is often the case with old roses.

Cornelia

[A subtle scent of musk]

The small semi-double flowers in bouquets of 'Cornelia' emit an agreeable, though musky, fragrance. They are a delicate peachy pink tinted with darker and lighter shades, and become truly apricot as they open. This color evolves over the months: paler in summer, it becomes vibrant in the last flowers of autumn, making this rose even more beautiful at the end of the season.

The shape of these roses, which bloom surrounded by many small buds of a darker pink tinged with yellow, is a very regular, somewhat loose cup that reveals its stamens. It evokes the camellia and certain carnations.

Its stems are purple with few thorns and the foliage is wonderful: elongated leaflets of a beautiful matte green to almost bronze, giving the shrub a somewhat somber look.

The passion for roses

'Cornelia' is one of the most beautiful roses of the '20s and one of the finest creations of the British Reverend H.J. Pemberton, who obtained it the very year of his death, 1925. He searched for musk-scented roses, the "true" perfume, he felt, of the old English varieties.

Among the progenitors of 'Cornelia' is the climbing and repeat-flowering rose, 'Trier,' for which Pemberton searched in Germany. It was frequently used in the early 1900s to develop musky hybrids. A great collector, he truly loved these flowers; they were his hobby and, later, his retirement. The minister told an American friend that he loved his roses so much "that there was no room in his heart for a wife!" He offered all his creations to his gardeners, John and Ann Bentall, who became caught up in their turn in the passion for roses.

It generously fills its space

'Cornelia' is a robust and healthy rose, and its supple branches provide it a light and airy posture. Wider than it is tall—and it can reach the height of a man—it generously fills its space. Throughout the season, new shoots will bud to assure that a profusion of small fragrant flowers will ornament the shrub.

Three years of regular pruning are necessary to shape this rose well. After that, cutting the ends of the branches will keep its beautiful balance.

It has good resistance to disease, so it isn't necessary to treat it.

A beautiful rose for semi-shade

Given its fullness, 'Cornelia' can easily stand alone, and even in semi-shade, it will give its very best.

It can also make a superb landscaped hedge when planted several stalks in a row, spaced about 40 inches (100 cm) apart. Try training it against a low trellis or railing that it will decoratively drape.

Whatever you decide, a show of perfect beauty is guaranteed, especially if you combine it with mauve perennials: asters, delphiniums, and pulsatillas, for example.

Hybridizer: *H. J. Pemberton*
Year: *1925*
Height: *5 to 6 feet (1.5–1.8 m)*
Group: *Clustered-flower bush*

Jacques Cartier

[Spirit of lavender]

This old rose gives off a wonderful strong fragrance of lavender. The flower is very doubled, in quarters characteristic of old roses: the small petals, short and very numerous, snuggle against each other; those that hide the stamens remain rolled tightly inward. This flower shape is also called a "rosette."

The rosebuds, opening out on stiff stems from a hollow of pointed sepals, emerge as beautiful flowers whose bright, soft pink darkens toward the center, the outer petals being almost white. Throughout the blooming, the whole flower continues to lighten, becoming completely colorless when the flowers are in full sun.

Their pale tone is warmed by a very green, deep, dense foliage—vigorous and tough—with characteristically pointed leaflets. At the end of the season, however, when the temperature drops and the sunshine dwindles, the flowers of 'Jacques Cartier' retain their deeper pink coloring.

Hybridizer:
Moreau-Robert
Year: *1868*
Height: *40 inches (100 cm)*
Group: *Large-flowered bush*

Hot recommendation

'Jacques Cartier' is a small bush that connoisseurs consider one of the most beautiful of all roses, and it is also one of the most interesting and easiest to grow of the old varieties.

Its growth is rapid and its firm branches give a nice erect bearing: to keep its beautiful compactness, cut it back by one third every spring.

It requires only a little care in order to repeat-flower throughout the summer: remove the wilted flowers, feed it regularly with rose fertilizer, and water it.

Reducing the number of buds in May will result in a repeat flowering with full splendor towards mid-August. And so long as it has enough to drink, the heat and the humidity will not bother it.

Near the house

With its small size and compact bearing, 'Jacques Cartier' is best in flowerbeds, placed where its fragrance can be most

This is the most beautiful of the 173 varieties created in the 19th century by rose growers from Anjou, Moreau and Robert. In their hybridization work they used a Portland rose brought from England by Josephine de Beauharnais to enrich her own remarkable rose nursery at Chateau de Malmaison, near Paris. That rose owes its name to the Duchess of Portland, who discovered it by accident in Italy in 1800, and brought it back with her. Its best quality, fortunately passed along to its descendants, is its habit of repeat flowering, meaning its ability to flower again several times, which is relatively rare in old varieties. 'Jacques Cartier' continues flowering all summer.
This variety is named in memory of the 16th century French navigator, the first explorer of Canada...or else it's an honor given to the amateur cultivator of roses at the end of the last century, Doctor Jacques Cartier.

appreciated. It is truly showcased when surrounded by perennials of all colors.

It can also form a landscaped hedge by spacing the stalks about 24 inches (60 cm) apart.

Maiden's Blush

Aura of myrtle

Hybridizer:
Unknown
Year: *18th century*
Height: *4.5 to 6 feet (1.4–1.8 m)*
Group: *Small shrub*

A name inviting reverie…and a fragrance that is sweet and captivating, like that of myrtle; these pretty, very double cup-shaped flowers are true old roses whose origin remains unknown.

The rounded cream-colored buds softly open their hundred petals to become a very short and puffy flower of a cameo pink, lighter on the edges and darkening toward the center. At the heart of these charming and delicate flowers is a veritable bud, small and elaborate.

The abundant foliage of this bush has very few thorns, and its shade varies between blue-green and gray-green.

The branches bend under the flowers

'Maiden's Blush' is a compact and vigorous rose. It is easy to grow, demanding very little, and is still found in many old gardens.

Its branches, often bending under the burden of the flowers, give the shrub a pleasing shape in complete accord with the charm of this very old variety. 'Maiden's Blush' tolerates just about any quality of soil and a variety of sun exposures, but it is most resplendent in full sun. Still, it isn't perfect: it flowers only once, during June and July. If you consider only two or three weeks of spectacular bloom an imperfection….

And it has others: the shrub can be mildly susceptible to slight attack by rust during prolonged dry spells. On the other hand, when the weather is too humid, the petals will probably be spoiled.

A garden classic

Most situations work for this rose and it remains a classic among old varieties. You should be able to find it without difficulty in catalogs or at the specialists'.

It is substantial enough to plant by itself, but you can also cluster three to five stalks to fill a large space. 'Maiden's Blush' will also form a beautiful landscaped hedge.

Cuisse de Nymphe or Maiden's Blush

The coloring of this flower is a true cameo pink, and its very suggestive name (literally "nymph's thigh" in French) reminds us that in earlier centuries the fashion was for very pale skin.

This rose is darker than its "sister," which merits its even more suggestive name in French, 'Cuisse de Nymphe Émue' (Nymph's Tender Thigh). That takes some doing!

'Maiden's Blush' is undoubtedly the most famous and most fragrant of the Alba roses immortalized by the Empress Josephine's painter, Pierre-Joseph Redouté.

In the course of its career—spanning centuries—this rose bore many other, certainly less poetic, names, but names that demonstrate all the same the charm rose growers have always found in it: Incarnata, Royal White Rose, The Royal, The Seductive, The Virginal….

To create a more free-form display, fill in a flowerbed of these large roses with more modern, shorter varieties with flowers of equally pastel tones. And to tie it all together, plant simple perennials with blue or pink flowers in the foreground. The effect will be utterly charming.

Heritage

[Floral and honeyed]

Hybridizer: *David Austin (Great Britain)*
Year: *1984*
Varietal Name: *'Ausblush'*
Height: *44 to 52 inches (110–130 cm)*
Group: *Large-flowered bush*

The fragrance of this English rose is unusual: it certainly evokes old roses, but in citrusy, peppery waves. It gives off iris, violet and geranium at once, with an added hint of honey. This refined perfume complements the perfect contours of the flower: a medium-sized cup shaped by very numerous tightly ruffled petals that permit a view of the golden stamen.

This is an old-style rose that is even more beautiful than old roses. Its coloring is a cameo pink, almost white on the outer petals and a bit darker at the heart. In certain growing conditions, this pink turns a pale salmon.

The flower is encircled by small, rounded, slightly pointed, darker buds. The foliage is a deep, rather shiny green.

In full sun

This rose is a beautiful shrub, robust, erect, and resistant to disease. Like many roses in this series, it requires a severe pruning to reinforce its spindly base. If neglected, it becomes lanky and far less prolific. It will repeat-flower, especially if you plant it in a sunny spot. In the shade, it has a tendency to thin out. Your 'Heritage' will appreciate an application of special rose formula fertilizer in the spring, and regular watering if the summer becomes dry.

Easy combinations

'Heritage' will form a beautiful arrangement of three or five bushes on their own, or in combination with other "English Roses" such as 'Abraham Darby' or 'Gertrud Jekyll.'

This planting will be complemented by a background of conifers, but its coloring also blends with gray foliage and blue flowers. Combine it with perennials in these tones. Should you prefer a monochrome palette, surround it with salmon-colored digitalis.

It can make a pretty hedge, the stalks being spaced approximately 24 inches (60

David Austin's English roses

*'Heritage' is a great classic in the family of
"English Roses" produced by David Austin.
In his eyes, it is his greatest success. It was
at the beginning of the 1960s that this
British grower began his selection work,
combining the cup shape and the almost
always perceptible perfume characteristic of
old roses with some qualities of modern
roses: a richer spectrum of colors, a longer
flowering and a greater resistance to
disease. Today, his collection boasts more
than 80 varieties, and many "old rose"
lovers admire them without suspecting that
they are in fact very recent creations. David
Austin had the luck to anticipate a trend
that led the work of other growers,
especially in France.*

cm) apart and pruned enough so that the
base fills out.

'Heritage' is a fragrant rose that you can
grow in a container; choose one deep
enough so it has room to grow. Placed on
a terrace, near the entrance or under the
windows, it will scent the area all summer.

Peppery rose

Hybridizer: *Meil-
land (France)*
Year: *1999*
Varietal Name:
'Meibderos'
Height: *32 to 36
inches (80–90 cm)*
Group: *Large-
flowered bush*

'Elle' exudes an intense perfume whose top note is peppery.

The pink color of this fabulous flower is a bit darker, with a light touch of yellow at the base of its petals and hints of violet giving it great distinctiveness.

The buds are full, light mauve and white, and open into double flowers with fifty overlapping petals that lighten as they age. The evolving character of color depends upon the climate.

A foliage of large shiny green leaflets shows off the profusion of roses whose petals in the end blow away, leaving the stems neat and tidy.

A modern rose

The rose 'Elle' is part of a new family offered only recently to gardeners who love fragrant roses that are easy to grow and beautiful to see, and are also fairly small and vigorous. 'Elle' is lovely in a small garden or a large container; it is demure and non-invasive.

These roses have an excellent resistance to disease and need very little treatment. Don't neglect them, though, or they won't fully bloom. They need good soil preparation before planting, regular pruning, watering and feeding, and protection from intense cold.

A cluster full of fragrance

'Elle' is one of the first roses to flower in the garden and it remains decorative until very late in the season.

Plant three stalks of this vigorous shrub in a triangle for a superb and fragrant cluster near the house. If you have only a terrace, plant 'Elle' in a pretty terra cotta pot or a square container made of wood or metal. Choose one that is deep enough, 16 to 20 inches (40–50 cm) or so, assuring good drainage with a bed of clay balls or broken pottery, and fill it with a blend of garden earth, rose potting mix and sand.

One or two 'Elle' roses in a bouquet will ensure an incredible scent.

A generous rose

'Elle,' one of the most recent creations of Alain Meilland, received an award for its perfume in the rose competition at Bagatelle in 1999. Its name is not as anonymous as it might seem: it is in fact that of the famous women's magazine. The sale of this rose benefits ALIS, an association created by Jean-Dominique Bauby for those afflicted with Locked-In Syndrome. Victimized by this condition (in which one is conscious and aware but unable to speak or move) as the result of a stroke, the former editor in chief of Elle magazine dictated a book entitled Le Scaphandre et le Papillon (The Diving Bell and the Butterfly) with blinks of his left eye before passing away in 1997. A portion of the sales of this rose is donated to the association, which has the purpose of helping the sick and their families. This rose was baptized during the Days of Plants in Courson in spring 1999.

The Whites

"I perfumed my soul

with the rose

for my entire life."

Guillaume Apollinaire

(1880-1918)

The pleasure of lily of the valley!

A delicious scent of lily of the valley emanates from the flattened double flowers of this soft cameo-colored rose, whose shape is typical of that of the famous Damask roses. Its frilly petals arranged in quarters little by little disclose their buff-beige stamens.

Waves of relatively large pale flowers cover this solid spreading rose from the month of May through late November. So long a flowering season, rare in old varieties, earns it the claim to be "perpetual."

The foliage has a soft look resembling that of primroses. It is abundant, matte, and gray-green, sometimes touched with purple. Botanists don't know why the reddish spots appear; they may be induced by environmental changes. In any case, they have no effect on the plant's growth.

A treasure born of chance

'Stanwell Perpetual' is one of those superb old varieties continuing to dwell in public and private gardens and to seduce rose lovers even today. Its exact origins are not known; there exist a number of different versions.
One version has it that this rose was produced in a garden in Stanwell, Scotland—fruit of the chance union of a Rosa pimpinellifolia *and a* Rosa x damascena semperflorens, *the latter having most certainly transmitted its gene for repeat flowering. For more than a century, it has been treasured for the length of its blooming.*
It was the British nurseryman Lee, a resident of Stanwell, who first sold 'Stanwell Perpetual' in 1838.

A graceful bearing, without stiffness

This is a graceful and vigorous rosebush, full and thorny, with thin arched branches that stretch out wider than they grow tall: they grow to about 5 feet (150 cm) in height before falling into wide arcs. It must therefore have enough space to grow uncrowded.

In three or four years, this robust shrub will be impenetrable. But it ages poorly: its principal stalks, covered with large thorns, have a tendency to turn gray. It must renew its wood regularly; this is achieved by cutting the thickest branches every year.

From its Scottish origins, 'Stanwell Perpetual' developed great ability to withstand all types of winter weather: it is hardy and insensitive to frost. It is also little bothered by the quality of soil, tolerating sandy and even slightly alkaline soils.

A foundation decoration

Requiring a large place to spread out, 'Stanwell Perpetual' works as the base for a flowerbed or as a hedge, spacing the stalks at least 20 inches (50 cm) apart. Just prune it lightly at the end of winter to trim those branches that are flimsy and are growing towards the center of the plant.

Gathered at the end of summer, the cut roses hold up well for four or five days—but be careful of the thorns!

Hybridizer: *Lee (Great Britain)*
Year: *1838*
Height: *5 to 6 feet (1.5–1.8 m)*
Group: *Large-flowered bush*

[The scent of citrus in the land of roses]

Hybridizer: *Meilland (France)*
Year: *1984*
Varietal name: *'Meimafris'*
Height: *36 to 48 inches (90–120 cm)*
Group: *Large-flowered bush*

The traditional scent of rose, lifted by hints of citrus and spice: such is the intense sophisticated fragrance of these large very double flowers that open into a very classic and opulent shape.

Their sixty-five overlapping petals have a delicate creamy white color with casts of pink, all of which is touched with the sheen of pearl, a delicacy of tones set off by a dense matte green foliage.

The flowering, which is early, repeats in autumn and continues until the first frosts of winter. But these delicate flowers can be spoiled by bad weather.

A vigorous rose

'Jardins de Bagatelle' is one of the new easy-to-grow generation of roses: it is a full bush that grows energetically and is not susceptible to disease, heat, or frost.

You can therefore plant it anywhere in a good fertilized soil and sunny location. Naturally, it requires the traditional maintenance of most roses: a pruning to tidy it up in autumn, a short shaping pruning in February or March, and feeding at the beginning of its growth to assure repeat flowering. In return, 'Jardins de Bagatelle' will impart its full splendor for many months.

A romantic rose

The delicate coloring of its petals makes 'Jardins de Bagatelle' a particularly romantic rose. Accentuate this aspect in a cluster of a few stalks—always odd in number—by adding a sculpture or other aesthetic element. A bench nearby will induce a feeling of rest in a sweetly scented environment.

In a corner reserved for cut flowers, 'Jardins de Bagatelle' brings the subtlety of white flowers with casts of pink. In a bouquet, they soften the more vivid shades of deep pink or red varieties, blending their perfume in a renewed harmony.

Homage to Bagatelle

Bagatelle, in the Bois de Boulogne in Paris, is a place of myth for rose lovers. When in 1905 Jean-Claude Nicolas Forestier, keeper of the parks and gardens of the city of Paris, asked for help to create what would become one of the most famous rose nurseries in the world, it was Jules Gravereaux himself, founder and proprietor of the Haÿ-les-Roses nursery, who gave him a quarter of his roses, some 1,500 varieties. From this first collaboration, the two men conceived the idea of an "international rose competition" and on the 2nd of July, 1907, the first gathering featured 148 varieties presented by 58 exhibitors. The exhibition quickly found worldwide fame and inspired similar competitions, but it remains the most prestigious.
In 1984, 'Jardins de Bagatelle' won a prize there for its perfume.

Margaret Merril

[The perfume of perfection]

Hybridizer: *Jack Harkness (Great Britain)*
Year: *1978*
Varietal name: *'Harkuly'*
Height: *32 inches (80 cm)*
Group: *Clustered-flower bush*

A soft and delicate traditional rose fragrance wafts from these pretty, waxy, white flowers touched with carmine. The perfectly-shaped buds are a shade of soft pink and they open into magnificent semi-double flowers whose white coloring brightens in the sun. They comprise about thirty petals, which are higher and pointed at the reddish heart, and have fully visible stamens.

These flowers are joined in clusters whose very pure coloring stands out against a luxurious dark green and very jagged foliage.

A beautiful vegetation

'Margaret Merril' is not particularly large, but it is truly superb—a bushy rose that lends a purity and fragrance to a flowerbed and deserves more availability to rose lovers.

The shrub is not very disease resistant: it's inclined to attack by mildew, black spot and rust. But well maintained, it presents little difficulty in scenting a garden for many weeks and its greenery pleases the eye. It also tolerates rather poor soil.

The darling of bees

Don't place 'Margaret Merril' near where people gather. It draws adoring bees!

In clusters or in flowerbeds, it combines appealingly with red and dark pink flowers, be they roses or other species. Use perennials or annuals which grow quickly and whose coloring emphasizes the purity of 'Margaret Merril.'

You can grow a lovely fragrant hedge by aligning several stalks. Always follow the maintenance imperatives: prune severely the first year, and follow it with a lighter pruning in subsequent years, all accompanied by a good fertilization.

'Margaret Merril' can very easily be cultivated in a pot or in a garden. Its cut flowers are marvelous in a bouquet blended with vivid tones.

The white rose—a symbol of purity

In the ancient Mediterranean world, it was believed that the rose was first white before becoming red, and myths abound to explain this: among them, those of Aphrodite, Adonis and Eros. In Christianity, the white rose became the symbol of the Virgin Mary and virginal purity, and is associated with many saints.

The War of the Roses, in which the two branches of the Plantagenets battled for the throne of England, led to the birth of the bi-colored rose in 1485; it united the white rose of the house of York with the red rose of the house of Lancaster.

In the language of flowers today, the white rose continues to evoke innocence and purity. To offer a white rose can also signify "I am worthy of you."

In the garden or in a mixed bouquet, white roses enhance the other colors, even the most pale. And when, like 'Margaret Merril,' they are wonderfully fragrant, they deserve a place at the forefront.

The Lilacs,
Violets
and Mauves

*"From each of these half-opened or fully bloomed
corollas comes fragrances as varied as the shapes
and colors of each species: musky scents reminiscent
of the Orient, languishing and languid scents, a sweet
breath like that of the vineyard in bloom, voluptuous
like kisses, soft like the first breeze of spring. Vision
and smell are intoxicated: and in the vibrant summer
light, a confused murmur of bees, bumblebees and
golden rose beetles make a harmonious accompani-
ment to the lilting music of the aromas and colors."*
André Theuriet—1902—

The Roses Cultivated at Haÿ in 1902

Senteur Royale

[A racy perfume!]

Hybridizer: *Tantau (Germany)*
Year: *1986*
Varietal name: *'Tanschaubud'*
Height: *4–6 feet (1.3–1.8 cm)*
Group: *Large-flowered bush*

These beautiful roses, whose name is not lightly given, are magnificently perfumed. The tall buds open into full and opulent very double flowers with a classic elegance, whose thick petals are a deep pinky-lilac, a distinctive color some call deep violet.

These flowers stand straight on long stems, each bearing a single bloom, which shines in all its splendor, emerging from a thick, deep, satiny foliage. This flowering repeats almost continually from spring to autumn.

A shrub to spruce up

Unfortunately, the shrub's bearing is not this rose's most valued quality. It's a robust bush, certainly, whose beautiful lofty stature does not fear frost or intense heat, but it falls prey easily to the diseases common to roses.

To get the most from the beauty of its flowers, 'Senteur Royale' demands to be coddled: each year, in March, apply a special magnesium-rich rose food and blend it into the top layer of soil, weed at the base to avoid the competition of weeds, treat it preventively for diseases and parasites every second or third week from April to October, and remove withered flowers.

A rose for cut flowers

'Senteur Royale' is a particular gem as a cut flower in bouquets.

In a small garden, try planting it as a standard: it is easier to care for in this form and its perfume will be at an advantageous height. You can place this rose tree in the middle of a bed of herbaceous perennials that will accentuate it without invading it. It can also be grown in a container at a good height to enjoy its fragrance.

Greenhouse roses

This creation by the German grower Tantau seduced noses from the very first, and took several top prizes for its perfume, notably at the competition in Baden-Baden. Although Tantau specialized mostly in greenhouse roses for cut flowers, he kept 'Senteur Royale' for gardens, its being too sensitive to adapt well to large-scale cultivation.

The florist roses cultivated in greenhouses must demonstrate great regularity of growth, a good resistance to disease, and produce salable flowers on tall stems the whole year through. Once cut, they must hold up well fairly long term, and they are tested to guarantee the satisfaction of clients. There exists today a great diversity in every shade and color, but very few are fragrant. For fragrance, nothing can compete with a bouquet of roses freshly cut from the garden.

[Mouth-watering]

Hybridizer: *Delbard (France)*
Year: *1996*
Varietal name: *'Delviola'*
Height: *32 to 36 inches (80–90 cm)*
Group: *Large-flowered bush*

The color of this flower, which ranges between rose and violet, is like the jam of well-ripened blueberries. It has a rich, gourmet fragrance: a fruity overtone evokes mandarin and citronella, then its floral note hints of hyacinth and lilac, before returning to fruity exhalations of passion fruit and mango.

The flowers of 'Chartreuse de Parme' are medium-sized and have a very pretty shape: their numerous shimmering petals are very tightly packed and lightly ruffled, giving them a flared look as they gently open.

The foliage is an incredible deep matte green whose hints of blue accentuate the color of the flowers.

Regular upkeep

'Chartreuse de Parme' is a rose whose semi-erect bearing requires some attention to be its most splendid: a regular application of compost in March or April and rose food in May and July; a good balanced watering all summer long; a very short pruning; and a good mulching. Its disease resistance is average and requires alertness to many changing factors—the placement of the plant, weather and soil conditions. A rose can be diseased one year and not another. In the case of marked sensitivity, treatment in the winter will help free it of all hibernating parasites.

Cut its wilted flowers so that they do not fall on their own; in exchange, it will reward you with many repeat flowerings throughout the season.

A touch of color

Plant 'Chartreuse de Parme' in beds or borders. Combine at least three stalks to create a touch of color, but if this rose seduces you and if you have the space, plant 30 or 40 of them. Your bed can also blend many varieties with the same style of flowers: 'Souvenir de Marcel Proust,' from the same family, with equally full and fragrant yellow flowers, is a lovely mix with the wonderful warm coloring of

The perfume of this rose has been awarded many prizes: at Bagatelle, Madrid, Geneva, and Baden-Baden in 1996. It was demonstrated at Bagatelle that the perfume of a rose is a vital function, like breathing, that could change throughout the day: at nine o'clock that day, the flowers of 'Chartreuse de Parme' gave off no perfume, to the great despair of its grower. One hour later they were "awakened," and sufficiently seduced the jury to win the prize. Like the yellow-flowered 'Souvenir de Marcel Proust,' this is a rose in the "Souvenirs d'Amour" ("Memories of Love," in English) family, an appellation chosen by the Delbard family for their roses with the re-discovered charm of yesteryear.

'Chartreuse de Parme.' But the gourmet aspect of these flowers could very well prompt you to plant it with small fruits: blackcurrants or currants.

The enchanted note

Its intense and sweet perfume, very fruity with a note of rose, persists whatever the conditions of temperature and humidity. For some it is intoxicating, but it is certain to enchant even the least trained noses.

The flowers are also remarkable: they are very large, a little over 5 inches (13 cm) in diameter, and endowed with some eighty ruffled petals that make them look like enormous peonies. When 'Yves Piaget' was created at the beginning of the 1980s, its shape was a minor revolution. Today, it is the height of style.

The color of this rose is dark lilac, specifically a shade called 'Neyron pink,' a nearly fluorescent reincarnation of the old rose by the name of 'Paul Neyron:' it is a dark pink suffused with silver.

As for its foliage, it is almost matte, and dark and gleaming.

This rose launched a new style

Here is another rose that has been highly prized from the very first: it received the cup for fragrance at Bagatelle among its many medals, notably at the Geneva competition, where its large peony shape intrigued visitors. Among these visitors was Yves Piaget, the Swiss jeweler, who expressed such great admiration for it that Alain Meilland chose to give the rose his name. In France, old-style roses were not yet the fashion, but after having seduced this famous Swiss, it went on directly to conquer the Germans, for whom it evoked the charm of Provence. Its success is indisputable.

Its charm requires some care

'Yves Piaget' is not very thorny, a robust plant that produces a veritable plague of large suckers. It does not withstand harsh climates; it thrives only in temperate regions. Be sure to till and mulch its base at the start of winter.

Be on guard for attacks by fungus: treat it preventively with an anti-fungal product for roses or a total rose treatment at regular intervals throughout the growth period.

And as with all vigorous roses, give it a long pruning at the end of winter.

Beautiful with blue

The large dark pink peonies of 'Yves Piaget' will be showcased by planting light flowers in shades of blue close by: sage, céanothes, or even a small rosemary bush. Low perennials with silvery foliage, like lambs' ear or cineraria, will also create a harmony of colors.

This is a good rose for cut flowers.

Hybridizer: *Meilland (France)*
Year: *1983*
Varietal name: *'Meivildo'*
Height: *32 to 44 inches (80–110 cm)*
Group: *Large-flowered bush*

Honorine de Brabant

[Deliciously old rose]

Hybridizer: *Unknown*
Year: *before 1900*
Height: *over 6 feet (1.8 m)*
Group: *Large-flowered bush or small climber*

These cup-shaped double flowers of lilac pink splashed with carmine and purple are endowed with a delicious perfume characteristic of old roses. Their original color becomes deeper, more alluring, and even more beautiful as the season draws to a close.

They are of medium size, with flowers 2.5 to 3 inches (6–8 cm) in diameter that first have a spherical shape and then spread in quarters as they open. The outer petals form a shell surrounding the smaller center petals.

These flowers are grouped in small bouquets among the abundant large leaves of the shrub, which are smooth, pointed, and a bit rough. The green stems bear a moderate number of very sharp, large thorns.

'Honorine de Brabant' will give off its scent especially after a gentle rain, but its silky petals will not bear a heavy shower well. This is one of the most prolifically flowering roses with variegated blooms: the branches quickly fall under their weight. This is also one of the rare old roses to have a second flowering in autumn.

A large vigorous bush

'Honorine de Brabant' is a large, vigorous and erect rose bush. It will quickly take up space, becoming as wide as it is tall, and requires as a result good space for it to spread out. Like all roses, it loves full sun, but it will tolerate a semi-shaded location.

This beautiful dense shrub is full of vitality and not especially susceptible to disease. The only imperatives are a regular pruning and a good application of compost and food.

Planted against a wall or other support, 'Honorine de Brabant' can also be grown as a climbing rose.

One is enough

Given the growth it will show in a few years, choose 'Honorine de Brabant' only if you have a large garden—and one plant will suffice!

Let it grow completely naturally or train it as a climber.

An unknown beauty

There is no trace of this variety in old books and its origin remains unknown. But it is very close to the Bourbon rose 'Commandant Beaurepaire,' which also has variegated flowers, and was obtained by the French rose growers Moreau and Robert in 1874. Few old roses wear such spotted "dresses."
Today, some growers, Delbard especially, search for this look, offering a small collection of these types of roses. His 'Roses de Peintres' ('Roses of the Painters') varieties have shimmering fiery colors in shades of yellow, pink, violet and red, which change from one flower to another, evolving throughout the day and throughout the duration of their blooming. These constantly varying effects make the flowers seem like renderings of the impressionists.... All this and they are fragrant too!

Pruning is important, especially for encouraging a second flowering: reduce the framework branches by one third, and at the end of the year remove the old wood. And cut back the wilted flowers religiously!

Dioressence

[Perfume of the master]

Hybridizer: *Del-bard (France)*
Year: *1984*
Varietal name: *'Deldiore'*
Height: *28 to 36 inches (70–90 cm)*
Group: *Large-flowered bush*

This rose bearing the name of Christian Dior's great perfume has an intriguing and very balanced fragrance, blending the scents of bergamot, geranium, and moss.

The flowers are equally sumptuous, with a beautiful cup shape and a very distinctive color: lilac with light purple on the under side of the petals. It comes close to blue, which many growers strive to attain. It's interesting to observe that, because nearly all the flowers of this shade are fragrant, the two genes responsible for these characteristics are quite probably connected.

In fact, this unusual color evolves as the flower blooms. The bud is a vibrant shade of blue, which lightens as the flower opens, passing through a whole spectrum of shades: violet, cardinal, then nearly white…while the long, warm-yellow stamen appears very quickly, creating a striking contrast. These large, tightly scrolled flowers are grouped in threes and fours. They give an impression of softness somewhere between classic and wild roses. More or less vibrant in color, those of a darker shade give the most intense perfume.

The satiny, medium-green leaves are fairly large.

Small wonder to coddle

'Dioressence' is a small well-balanced bush whose flowers are abundant and marvelously perfumed. However, it demands regular attention in order to remain in top form.

From its planting, you must coddle and watch it like a fragile beauty who will appreciate your lavish care and attention. But what a joy when it puts forth all the uniqueness of its color and the intensity of its perfume!

Don't neglect regular applications of fertilizer during the growing period, watering if the weather is dry, and preventive treatments against fungal diseases that may lie in wait for 'Dioressence.'

The rose in the perfume industry

The perfume Dioressence is a great classic of the house of Christian Dior, launched in 1979, under the name with which Delbard baptized one of his most original creations five years later.

It's entirely natural that the rose be associated with perfumes, and of all flowers, it has certainly been the preference of perfume-makers for more than three thousand years. The roses used in the perfume industry today are most often botanical varieties grown for this purpose in but a few countries—Turkey, Romania, Iran, and Morocco—as well as in France, in the region of Grasse. They are treated on site by one of two methods: distillation by water, rendering rose water and essential oil; or distillation by volatile solvents, which leaves the extract called rose absolute. The oil retains the fresh and fruity qualities essential to the making of great perfumes, but absolute, which is heavier, can also give interesting effects.

A beautiful mass effect

'Dioressence' is a difficult rosebush to blend with others, but it gives a superb effect in a bed of several stalks of this one variety. You can enliven the display by combining it with orange-yellow roses, such as the superb 'O Sole Mio,' from the same grower, whose light perfume blends nicely with the exhalations of 'Dioressence.'

Grown with much care in a corner of the garden, 'Dioressence' is excellent for cut flowers to scent and give a touch of originality to your bouquets.

Mamy Blue

[Intense femininity]

Hybridizer: *Delbard (France)*
Year: *1991*
Varietal name: *'Delblue'*
Height: *32 to 36 inches (80–90 cm)*
Group: *Large-flowered bush*

Despite its very cool color, 'Mamy Blue' is a very feminine rose with a warm and intense perfume. The first soft notes of citronella are completed by a somewhat heady perfume of geranium and ylang-ylang, before fading with exhalations of violet, hay and heliotrope.

The buds are tightly scrolled and the large, very doubled flowers have a perfect shape, both classic and conventional.

As for their color, it is remarkable: a vibrant mauve with blue reflections, whose shade evolves as the flower opens. The hue at first evokes certain autumn skies, then takes on reddish flashes as it blooms.

A "mamy" to pamper

'Mamy Blue' is a rosebush of average size and vigor that demands to be well cared for to give full satisfaction.

Plant it in full sun, in a hole enriched with planting soil, and prune it very short,

especially in the first years, to give it a balanced shape. Apply fertilizer regularly, water it abundantly if the weather is dry, and above all watch for the first attacks of disease. 'Mamy Blue' is susceptible to black spot, a fungus which causes black spots to appear on the leaves, and which proliferates in heat, rain or nozzle waterings, sometimes to the point of completely defoliating the shrub. You will find rose anti-disease sprays in specialty shops. They allow you to prevent or end the disease.

This rose may repeat flower at the end of summer.

A beautiful cut flower

'Mamy Blue' is worthy of planting all on its own: three, five, or even a single plant is enough to assure you an eye-catching display. Its color is not easy to blend, but it can be highlighted by the proximity of yellow roses, such as the luminous 'Souvenir de Marcel Proust' or 'O Sole Mio,' from the same grower. You can also

The myth of the blue rose

For a very long time, many growers have dreamed of creating a blue rose. Despite its name, 'Mamy Blue' is not actually this shade that many other flowers in nature bear. The explanation is biological: roses are unable to produce delphinidine, the blue pigment in flowers. No grower can ever attain it naturally, and the promises of some catalogs are only an illusion achieved by retouching the photos.

There does exist however a way of creating a blue rose and the Australians were the first to suggest it: this would be a genetically modified rose, with the introduction of a gene from another flower carrying the capacity to synthesize delphinidine in the heart of rose cells.

opt for other yellow species, such as a border of *Bidens* or a golden yarrow.

This is a beautiful flower for cutting, as it holds up for ten to fifteen days. A 'Mamy Blue' rose in a pretty vase all by itself is a wonderful fragrant bouquet.

Lavender Dream

[A unique scent]

Hybridizer: *Inter-plant (Holland)*
Year: *1984*
Varietal name: *'Interlav'*
Height: *32 to 40 inches (80–100 cm)*
Group: *Country rose*

The unique scent of 'Lavender Dream' combines all at once notes of citrus, mimosa, lily of the valley and lilac, with an added touch of grass and heliotrope…and this perfume is perceptible, at certain times of the day, from far away, without having to bring your nose to the small flat flowers.

Immediately opened from their buds, the young flowers of 'Lavender Dream' are a pretty pink color which turns to lavender blue as they bloom, becoming more and more mauve as they age. These are semi-double flowers, which have only two rows of petals, too few to hide their golden stamens. A profusion of flowers inundates this rosebush from June to October, going so far as to hide the small, shiny light green leaves.

Easy to grow

Here is a rose that is particularly easy to grow: it doesn't fear frost or heat, and doesn't require any pruning except a severe cutting back every two or three years. Cutting the branches back halfway will force it to fill out, encouraging a more abundant flowering.

It is not entirely disease resistant, though; a preventive spray with an all-purpose product will help you protect it from attack by fungus and other pests.

As a groundcover or in a pot

'Lavender Dream' will make an attractive fragrant bed: to give it fullness, plant at least a dozen stalks in staggered rows, spaced about 40 inches (100 cm) apart. Surrounded by grass, it produces a superb natural effect: its low branches spread like a groundcover. Clearing the center with a few cuts from your pruning shears balances the growth of this shrub.

Space the stalks of 'Lavender Dream' farther apart in a row to delineate a more traditional hedge of conifers with its color and perfume, or as a similar border for a planting of old roses.

A country rose

This is a Dutch rose, a creation of the firm Interplant, founded by the nursery specialist Ilsink. It too has received a number of medals in international competition, among them, the prize at Bagatelle, France, in the category of country roses, newly instituted in 1986 to award and promote wild roses commercialized for less than six years. The criteria for country roses and traditional rosebushes are vastly different. The latter are judged for the uniqueness of the flowers aloft their elegant stems. A country rose is judged for vigor, resistance to disease, and the profuseness and duration of its flowering. 'Lavender Dream' is one of the few country roses to have a fragrance, making it a noteworthy specimen in its category, and the only one in this collection.

This rose gives equal splendor when grown in a pot, and it can nicely dress up a spot on the terrace. In the course of winter cleaning, tie up its supple branches—they will form a flowering cascade at the return of spring.

Symphony of fragrances

Hybridizer:
François Dorieux (France)
Year: *1995*
Varietal name: *'Dorient'*
Height: *40 to 48 inches (100–120 cm)*
Group: *Large-flowered bush*

'Mélodie Parfumée' ('Melody Perfume' or 'Perfumed Melody') combines an intense fragrance—very citrusy and spicy, with a top note of clove—with an extraordinary, truly unique color that evolves through the flower's life from violet purple to silvery mauve.

The buds are medium sized and elegantly shaped, their shade varying between purple and violet. They bloom into flowers of 3 to 4 inches (8–10 cm) in diameter and some thirty-odd petals. The blossoms open into a rather flat form evocative of the camellia.

They emerge from a beautiful, very dense matte green foliage. And when they fade, the petals fall on their own, leaving the branches of the rosebush clean.

Remarkable vigor

When he discovered a rose with so many qualities so rare among its peers, François Dorieux understood its value very quickly…and selection of 'Mélodie Parfumée' was much more rapid than usual.

Aside from this variety's original color and intense and long-lasting perfume, the vegetation of this rose is remarkable in health and vigor. Its flowering is prolonged and abundant.

The only constraints are the mandate for a regular pruning at the end of winter and a close watch for disease throughout the season.

Marriage in white

A few 'Mélodie Parfumée' roses, always in uneven numbers, form a beautiful bed on their own, but they also integrate well into a landscaped décor.

Mixing them with tall white or yellow flowered perennials, such as varieties of anthemis, aster, day-lily, and iris, will show off their color.

Once cut, the flowers of 'Mélodie Parfumée' do not keep, but just a few in a bouquet will scent an entire room and add a brief note of amazing color.

A rose that inspires artists

Having captivated him with its extravagant and unusual scent and color, Firmenich, a Swiss perfume maker based in Geneva, selected this rose on the occasion of his one-hundredth birthday. His company, founded in 1895 and the fourth largest of its kind in the world, is a supplier chiefly to the food and beverage industries, makers of soap and detergent, and major perfume manufacturers. It was he who baptized the variety 'Mélodie Parfumée.' Firmenich chemically synthesized the essence of this rose in a perfume that he reserved for select clients. But this flower has inspired not only a perfumier: French musician Jean Musy took it upon himself to compose a symphony in its honor, evoking in the space of about twelve minutes all the richness of its perfume as expelled over the hours of the day. A veritable "perfumed melody!"

The Yellows and Oranges

"I adore roses, they are the daughters of God and man, delicious country beauties of whom we have been able to make incomparable princesses."

George Sand (1804-1876)

Abraham Darby

[A whole orchard in a rose]

Hybridizer: *David Austin (Great Britain)*
Year: *1985*
Varietal name: *'Auscot'*
Height: *40 to 60 inches (100–150 cm)*
Group: *Large-flowered bush*

'Abraham Darby' is a rose whose perfume is reminiscent of an orchard, with waves of citronella and rose accented by the scents of grapefruit and apricot, cinnamon and clove.

This sumptuous rose is from the family of "English Roses;" they blend the shape and scent of old roses with the disease resistance and repeat flowering of modern roses. Its flowers are enormous cups with fully visible stamens and abundant curling petals that blend shades of yellow, pink and apricot. Their color is deeper in the center and more pale at the edges.

The flowers bloom against a true green foliage and often bend under their own weight at the tip of the petiole, giving this rose a tender charm.

Good growth, good maintenance

'Abraham Darby' is a large robust bush, but its shape generally lacks fullness and so it tends to become rather lanky. A few strategic snips with the pruning shears in early spring will assure its pleasing proportions. It can also be trained as a climber.

Like all the roses in this series, 'Abraham Darby' demands good maintenance: planting in enriched soil, regular applications of compost and fertilizer, abundant, repeated watering, a good mulching and regular checking for pests and disease. Faithful performance of this routine will guarantee long seasons of superb flowering.

A short pruning the first two years strengthens the plant, making it much less crucial later.

An impeccable allure

A nice bed is created with three to five of these roses in a sunny spot; space them 24 inches (60 cm) apart. Use this variety alone or mix it with other roses by David Austin whose coloring will blend harmoniously.

A bouquet of cut flowers

These soft-colored charming flowers create romantic bouquets. So that they keep as long as possible, cut them early in the morning and place them immediately in a pail of water to which is added a cut flower preservative (available at florists, garden shops, and supermarkets). This will allow the stems to fill with water. Then arrange your bouquet. Change the water daily and remember to add floral preservative each time to prolong the life of your bouquet.
When the flowers begin to fade, you can revive them by "electroshock:" submerge the base of the stems in boiling water, and, keeping them under water, cut a half an inch off the bottom, and then place them immediately in cool water.

'Abraham Darby' is also attractive at the rear of a flowerbed or trained against a wall. In fact, here it might even give its best appearance.

It is also a good variety as a cut flower.

Agnes

[Musk or citronella?]

Hybridizer: *Saunders (Canada)*
Year: *1922*
Height: *over 6 feet (1.8 m)*
Group: *Large shrub*

Here is an exceptional old rose with graceful pale yellow flowers whose intriguing and original fragrance shifts between musk and citronella.

The ochre-colored buds open into very double flowers with the shape of an old rose. Their rare color—amber yellow—turns to white with age. Quite loose around the edges, the small thin petals gather at the center, enclosing the stamens.

The flowers are very plentiful in spring, during their first flowering, and they return intermittently throughout the summer when the shrub is well planted. When left in place, the flowers transform in autumn into small red fruits that remain very decorative.

This large shrub, adorned with small, embossed leaves of medium green, delicately arches its thorny stems.

A truly rugged rose

'Agnes' inherited the wonderful vigor of *Rosa rugosa* of which it is a hybrid, and is particularly easy to grow. It is a robust shrub with an erect and bushy bearing

A happy hybrid

It was the Canadian grower, Saunders, who had the idea in the 1920s of crossing a Rosa rugosa—*the rugged rose of China and Japan characterized by a strong vegetation and large fragrant flowers—with the* Rosa foetida Persiana, *a rose with vibrant yellow flowers but an unpleasant scent (as the name indicates), which was brought from Iran a century earlier. He thus obtained a very original rose, having inherited from its "mother"—*Rosa rugosa—*its bearing and its thorns, and from its "father"—*Rosa foetida—*the form and color of its flowers. This is one of the rare hybrids of* Rosa rugosa *with yellow flowers. As for its perfume, 'Agnes' graciously made a delicate and agreeable synthesis of its parents. Saunders worked in a region with very harsh winters, so it is not surprising that his roses are famous for their hardiness and resistance to cold.*

that tolerates semi-shade and thrives in any soil, even light and sandy ones. In fact, it's one of the rare yellow roses not to suffer from poor soil. It manages on seashores, and thanks to its Canadian origins, it even handles a range of conditions from warm summers to harsh winters. It also shows a good resistance to wind. One weakness: its proneness to rust, which requires that it be closely monitored.

To encourage its rapidly filling out and blanketing its thorny stems with foliage, give 'Agnes' a severe pruning the first few years after planting. Later, you need only thin out the shrub and remove the old wood, maintaining its shape and proportions.

A rose for large gardens

A single bush of 'Agnes' is sure to enhance any garden. Just be careful not to place it too close to traffic: its thorns present a certain hazard.

It's a lovely foundation for a bed, combined with other shrubs or perennials: its pale yellow is very soft and works well with all other shades of flowers.

Consider this very thorny variety for a hedge that is both beautiful and impenetrable.

Jules Verne

[Very simply, a rose]

Hybridizer: *Michel Adam (France)*
Year: *1999*
Varietal name: *'Adecohuit'*
Height: *32 to 40 inches (80–100 cm)*
Group: *Large-flowered bush*

The very recent creation of a French grower, this rose has everything: a true rose fragrance—fruity and heady—a good resistance to disease, a repeat flowering from May to the frosts, and exquisite buttery flowers. Does it get any better than this?

The buds of 'Jules Verne' are egg-shaped and very elegant, opening into flowers 6 inches (15 cm) across with some thirty elliptical petals. The yellow heart is fringed with carmine pink, and these splendid shades lighten as the flower matures.

The flowers are single on their branches at the first flowering, then they group together, forming inflorescences. They emerge continually, from May to the first frosts of autumn, from a superb dark green, shiny foliage.

A dream of a rose

A great science fiction and fantasy writer, Jules Verne endowed the dreams of generations. And the rose that bears his name is likewise a dream: a vigorous bush with erect bearing, great vegetation and a particular resistance to cold and mildew.

'Jules Verne' keeps a healthy appearance even if you neglect the recommended disease controls. Regular pruning maintains its vigor and creates a balanced shape, but be careful not to prune so short as to weaken the plant. Throughout the growing season, keep up with regular hoeing, watering, and fertilizing, without which even vigorous and resistant roses will not thrive.

A rose that scents the whole house

Cut at the right moment, when the first petals begin to pull away, the blooms of 'Jules Verne' will last for up to a week in fresh water. It's rare for a fragrant rose to perform so well as a cut flower. And its scent endures for a long time, filling the entire house.

Homage to Jules Verne

It was at the Nantes Flower Show in 1999 that Michel Adam baptized his new rose in honor of Jules Verne, born in that very town in 1828. Jean-Jules Verne, great-grandson of the writer, attended the small ceremony, and deeply regretted not having a garden of his own in which to plant this beauty. Aside from the family's blessing, it was necessary to obtain authorization from the famous restaurant in the Eiffel Tower, which bears the same name and is longtime possessor of the Jules Verne trademark. From its first official presentation, this rose took the gold—recognition that omens well for long-term popular success in gardens everywhere.

In the garden as well, 'Jules Verne's' fruity fragrance attracts attention from afar. Plant it in clusters of five, even ten if you have room, or just a single plant, accented by plants of smaller size.

Sutter's Gold

[Glistening flowers]

Bush Hybridizer:
Swim (United States)
Year: *1949*
Height: *28 to 40
inches (70–100 cm)*
Group: *Large-
flowered bush*
**Climber
Hybridizer:** *Weeks*
Year: *1953*
Height: *8 to 13 feet
(2.5–4 m)*

The magnificent buds of this Hybrid Tea rose are flamboyant orange—a color sometimes called Indian red. They open quickly into elegant, large, fragrant double flowers.

The flowers are some thirty long, overlapping petals of a light yellow orange, with red and scarlet veins that pale as the flower fades. The petals then fall on their own, leaving the shrub clean.

The stems of 'Sutter's Gold' are smooth and its foliage is a healthy medium green, but a bit straggly. This is one of the earliest roses to flower, and it does so with exuberance.

Robust, yet shy

'Sutter's Gold' can grow with vigor, but it needs a bit of coaxing; without it, the shrub can have a rather stunted, thin appearance. Its resistance to disease isn't perfect, either.

This rose is most successful when it receives the requisite time and care: pruning at the end of winter, fertilizing at the beginning of spring and after the first flowering, and faithful preventive treatment with an all-purpose product for roses, including an anti-fungal and a pesticide for aphids. Your reward will be its fragrant, golden flowers.

'Sutter's Gold' comes also as a climber and this form is much more hardy and generous, and even disease resistant. The trade-off: it is much less prone to repeat flower.

A sea-rose by the shore

'Sutter's Gold' resists intemperate weather and thrives in coastal environments. There—or anywhere—plant it in a flowerbed or along the border of a lawn, grouping three or five plants together.

If you like to combine different species, consider violet tones that contrast artfully with yellow: sweet Williams, bellflowers, irises. But don't plant them so close to the rose as to constrict their growth.

Golden

*'Sutter's Gold' is the
California creation of
Herbert Swim. It was
obtained in 1949 and
presented the following
year by Armstrong, the
famous American nursery.
Very quickly embraced by
enthusiasts, it continues to
be widely cultivated, in its
bush as well as its
climbing form, obtained a
few years later through
mutation.*

*It was named on the
centenary of John A.
Sutter's discovery of gold
in the American River,
outside Sacramento,
California.*

*Throughout its competitive
career, 'Sutter's Gold'
collected medals and
awards chiefly in
recognition of its beautiful
flower, and especially its
perfume. Unfortunately,
the shrub itself lacks a
similar allure.*

Souvenir de Marcel Proust

[A walk in the garden]

An initial whiff of citronella, then fruity notes of apricot and pear, and a finish with a woody base of sandalwood and cedar! The complexity and the persistence of this perfume, whose subtleties press on the awareness with each return to it, strongly evoke childhood memories of the gardens in our past.

Many specialists hold that the scent and color of a rose should be congruent, and here is a rose that is just that: the fragrance of this yellow rose is mostly citrus.

The generous flower of an intense luminous yellow, with a shape as romantic as its name, has the striking charm of old cabbage roses. Its plentiful petals enfold and embrace each other as if to safeguard something precious at their center.

The leaves of soft yellow green are in perfect keeping with the perfume and color of these blooms.

Memory, memory

This rose has won numerous international competitions, notably the international grand prize for fragrance at Nantes in 1995.

Delbard classifies 'Souvenir de Marcel Proust' in the family "Souvenirs d'Amour" ("Memories of Love"). These voluptuous, romantic roses accord thoroughly with the traditional French notion of a garden.

Their flowers possess the best of both old and modern rose varieties: they are very full and generous globes with delicate color and delicious perfume, and they enjoy a long repeat flowering.

'Souvenir de Marcel Proust' gives pleasure with its warm inviting color, its full shape, and especially its perfume, evocative of the sweetest childhood nostalgia.

A cluster in full sun

'Souvenir de Marcel Proust' is a hardy, medium-sized shrub that branches well. In summer it will yield golden flowers so long as you provide the needed care: a short classic pruning in February, organic food in March and rose fertilizer during the growing season, a good watering when the weather is dry, and the prompt removal of wilted flowers.

Its resistance to disease is not guaranteed: regular preventive treatment beginning in February is always strongly recommended.

A romantic bed

'Souvenir de Marcel Proust' is ideal for creating a bed, but even a few plants of this variety alone will liven up an area.

You can combine it too with other roses having the similar old rose shape but different colors and scents—try the 'Comtesse de Segur,' another variety from the same grower; it has large dark pink pompon flowers and an essentially fruity fragrance.

This is also a good rose for cut flowers. Grow it in a secluded corner where the regular cutting of blooms will not diminish the garden's splendor.

Hybridizer: *Delbard (France)*
Year: *1992*
Varietal name: *'Delpapy'*
Height: *32 to 36 inches (80–90 cm)*
Group: *Large-flowered bush*

The Keys *to* Success

1. The choice

We have just described fifty of the most fragrant roses, but there are more than a thousand varieties for sale in nurseries. The choice is clearly vast. Choose your roses for the qualities you seek. Do you want an easy-to-grow plant that will become a beautiful shrub with the added beauty of flowers and fragrance during the summer months? Or are you prepared to dedicate the time and care necessary to a plant that will gratify you for only a few weeks, but with a more delicate blossoming? Certain varieties can be more difficult to find than others—the search may entail a veritable quest!

2. Buy your rose

Autumn is an ideal time, but in most areas, spring may be the only time that roses are available.

Whether you purchase your rose by mail order or through a nursery, it will normally be a bare root specimen: a few leafless branches the thickness of a pencil with no shoots at the level of the graft and no broken roots, revealing their good health. The roots will be wrapped in some moist protective material and placed in a carton or plastic bag for shipping, with an informational label giving its name, a photo of the flower, and some advice. Roses purchased in a shop are packaged bare root or in a pot and are ready to plant.
There are also roses cultivated in pots that are sold with their leaves, if not their flowers. These can be planted all year through.

3. Preserve your roses before planting

If you cannot plant your roses immediately after purchase, take precautions to preserve them in the best condition.
If they have bare roots and it will be only a few days, cover the roots with peat or sand in a box or a bucket, sheltered from frost. If it will be longer, bury them in a trench: release the branches that are bundled and place the plant in a shallow trench, sheltered along a wall. Cover the roots almost completely with light soil before watering them. If the roots are tightly packed, you can leave your roses as is for a few days in a cool place. If for longer than a week, open the ball and moisten the branches by spraying them every two days. It's ideal to soak the bare roots in water for 24 hours prior to planting.

4. Ensure a good understock

Many commercially produced roses are grafted, but many landscape and shrub roses are grown on their own roots. The upper part, or scion, is well-identified—it produces the flower you choose. But the understock is the foundation: it ensures the plant's healthy growth and enables less vigorous varieties to bloom more freely.
In the U.S., most commercially produced roses are grafted on two types of understock, 'Rosa Manettii' and 'Rosa Dr. Huey.' A smaller number, grown mostly for the warmest climates (e.g., Florida), are grafted on 'Rosa x Fortuneana.' Such information is not usually printed on the label.

Generally, this doesn't pose a problem since they are selected for maximum adaptability. But in certain cases, the understock can make a difference. A nursery specialist in your area will be able to help you with the specifics of climate and soil conditions.

5. Choose the place

While roses generally prefer sunny locations, placed strategic to the prevailing wind: it disperses their fragrance and they can act as a windscreen. Placed near the house or in the yard, your fragrant roses will be easily accessible. But consider planting a few bushes somewhere less conspicuous for cutting.

6. Analyze your soil

If it's only a matter of a few bushes, good soil too fussy about soil conditions, but some varieties can be a little sensitive. Consequently, it doesn't hurt to know the condition of your soil—alkaline or acid, heavy or light, clayey or sandy, rich or weak in trace elements.

7. Prepare the site for your roses

To maximize your chances for success, begin to prepare the site for your stones and debris. Enrich the soil at the base with an organic enriching agent purchased at a garden store—if the soil is alkaline (chalky), add 7 to 10 ounces (200–300 g) of powdered sulfur per square yard; then let it rest for a few weeks.

8. Prepare your rose for planting

Untangle the roots of the rose from the packing

fortunately, some will thrive in semi-shade. Avoid however any place receiving less than four or five hours of sunlight daily or having poor air circulation, such as a courtyard or passageway between tall houses. And remember, roses don't like the opposite, either—full sun exposure in front of a wall will likewise take the bloom off a rose.
Fragrant roses can be most appreciated when

preparation and regular use of enriching and fertilizing agents should suffice. If your projects are more ambitious—say, several large beds—you might want to do a soil analysis.
Soil samples taken from the garden will go to a special laboratory that will return a chemical analysis in a few weeks, accompanied by suggestions for improving it.
In general, roses are not

roses three to four weeks before planting so that the soil is well aerated and packs itself naturally. This preparation is all the more crucial when the soil quality is mediocre. If a rose has ever previously occupied the chosen site, it is imperative that you renew the soil to a depth of at least 16 inches (40 cm). Dig it up and sort through it, removing all the weeds and undesirable plants, as well as the

material. Freshen them up by lightly trimming the tips and stems. Then thoroughly soak the entire root system in water for up to 24 hours prior to planting. Should the roots dry out, the future vigor of the plant may be in jeopardy.
Preparation of ready-to-plant roses requires only a good moistening of the planting medium around the roots: submerge it in water for 15 minutes and

then lightly trim the rose's roots.

As for potted or container roses, soak them thoroughly to moisten the planting medium.

9. Put your rose in the ground

Fill the bottom of the hole with a prepared mixture of garden soil and food. At a good depth, arrange the bare roots in a star shape in the soil, respect-

with the soil.

If planting takes place in autumn, mound some soil about 4 inches (10 cm) deep around the graft union to protect it from cold, removing it in spring when danger from frosts has passed.

10. Plant your rose bed

Place your chosen roses in staggered rows to avoid a rectangular alignment, and plant three, five, or

most, around a majestic tree…and of course near the house. Don't forget that beds of fragrant large-flowered rose bushes should be seen close up, unlike plantings of grouped flowers, which can be farther away.

11. Plant your climbing rose

Climbing roses develop long branches that grow on a support.

airflow and prevent disease in some of the more sensitive varieties, maintain about 4 inches (10 cm) between the wall and the branches by mounting a wooden or plastic trellis on brackets. If planting against a wall, space the stem about 12 inches (30 cm) away, with the roots facing in the opposite direction.

ing their natural direction. The graft union must be placed at the level of the soil or just slightly below it.

Then fill in the hole, seeing that the soil mixture penetrates the roots well, without leaving any empty spaces. Pack the soil so that the rose stands very firm, and then water thoroughly. If the rose is in ready-to-plant mixture, place it (after having soaked it in water) so that the grafted point is level

seven (or more for a very large bed) of the same variety to create the effect of mass.

Avoid mixing too many colors if you want the impact of large splashes of color.

Avoid planting a bed in the middle of a lawn, especially a round bed: today's garden aesthetic rejects this. Plant along a walkway, beside some steps, in front of a hedge, in a passageway where you can see and smell it

Traditionally, the fragrant climbing rose mounts the wall of a house and thus grows within reach of hand and nose. But it's also a pleasing sight dressing up the side of an outbuilding, garden shed or pergola. In the center of the garden or along a walkway, you can grow it on an upright stake or double arch. And you can't go wrong training it on a fence—closed or open-weave.

To ensure adequate

12. Create a rose hedge

Consider whether you want a decorative hedge or a defensive one intended to prevent the passage of people or animals. If the latter, choose a very thorny rose whose effect will be even more dissuasive if you install not one, but two staggered rows. Don't forget, though, that this hedge will be bare in winter. To diminish this bareness, mix in a few evergreen bushes or double the hedge with a row of conifers.

The distance between each plant depends upon the anticipated growth of the adult shrub but in no case should it be less than 20 inches (50 cm). Stick with those varieties resistant to disease and pests.

The soil having been prepared as for individual roses above, you can even dig a simple trench.

gives a better overall effect.

As a precaution, plant in relative isolation any rose you know is prone to disease.

All the branches must receive sufficient light to develop well so as not to become centers of infection.

Certain gardeners advise keeping a distance of at least 6 feet (2 m) between each rose, using other

than in the ground, a container rose needs regular watering, fertilizing, and protecting from extreme cold. And keep in mind that the strong, direct rays of the sun on the sides of the pot can burn the roots.

Miniature roses, on the other hand, need less depth and can even be planted in a window box. Unfortunately, there are no fragrant miniature

ments to guarantee a balanced structure (for example, composted vegetable peels.)

A store of well-balanced compost can restore water and food to the roots. Low-cost commercial compost is almost entirely peat; before use, it must be mixed with other elements to give it the right balance. Choose a more expensive compost formulated specifically for

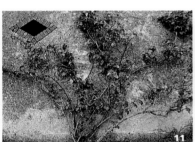   

13. Sufficiently space your roses

The distance between the plants depends on the effect desired and the expected vigor of the varieties selected. It varies from 20 inches (50 cm) in all directions for an average rose intended for a bed to 40 inches (100 cm) for a large shrub—especially landscape, climbing or standard roses.

Except to create a straight hedge, plant your roses in staggered rows, as this

plants to fill in the space between.

14. Plant your rose in a pot

In a small garden or courtyard, on a terrace or balcony, a potted rose is always right. Your taste and budget decide all else—just assure a minimum depth of 16 inches (40 cm) so that the rose can grow properly. A hole for drainage at the bottom and a drainage layer are also necessary. Even more

varieties, at least not to our knowledge.

15. Choose a good compost

The compost not only anchors the roots, it provides their nourishment—their very environment. With a base of peat, it includes manure or other enriching agents that supply the necessary microbes, the eventual fertilizing substances (first contributions to nourish the plant), and the ele-

roses; it will simplify your task, as it is ready to use.

16. Install a rose tree

The hole for planting a tree is prepared the same as for a bush, only that it must allow room for a stake, which is put in place before the rose. Depending on the variety of the graft, the habits of these "rose trees" will differ: some erect like rose bushes, some drooping like rose shrubs, others cascading like climbing roses. Planted in the center of a perennial flowerbed or along a walkway, rose trees enhance small gardens where trees would overwhelm.

Prune them the same as grafted roses at soil level, making sure that the branches kept are even so as to give an attractive shape.

One distinct advantage of a fragrant rose tree: they

prune—that they are still legible.

There are also less obtrusive metal and plastic labels upon which you can put the desired information. Be sure not to attach it so tightly that it strangles the stem as it thickens, or so high that you cut it away inadvertently when you prune. For even greater assurance, keep a planting layout of your roses on

too acidic, such as heath-peat.

A familiarity with the soil in your garden will allow you to improve it by enriching it with peat, lime, and organics, such as manure and compost. Failing that, you may still be able to cultivate one or two well-chosen roses, but you will never have a rose garden.

development of a damaging fungus if it comes into contact with the roots. Use commercial manure prepared for this purpose. Manure, seaweed, guano, and other diverse materials are the bases for a variety of composts. All of them can be used without restriction. Or you may prefer compost made from your own vegetable waste.

bring the flowers to your nose.

17. Label your roses
Don't forget to label your roses when you plant them. At the beginning, you're sure to know their names, but a few years later....

Roses, especially protected varieties, often bear weather-resistant labels made of wood or laminated paper. Check each year—say, when you

paper or on the computer.

18. Improve the soil
A newly planted young rose requires a loose, well-aerated soil sufficiently rich in organic elements that its roots can take off. A rose that starts off poorly rarely becomes a choice subject. Even if they are not very demanding, roses fear extremes: a soil too clayey and too heavy, or one sandy and very dry, too alkaline or

19. Apply enriching agents
A good quantity of organic enriching agents is even more imperative in planting than food or fertilizer. It softens soils that are too heavy, it gives substance to soils that are too light; to both, it adds the necessary microorganisms.

If you use manure, be sure it's not fresh. Fresh manure cannot decompose and can cause the

20. Apply fertilizer
A rose demands organic materials and minerals, its specific requirements differing with the variety. Regular applications of fertilizer support the vigor of the shoot, the abundance and duration of the flowering, and the resistance to disease and pests. But an excess is as damaging as a deficiency, so always use the recommended amount.

Don't fertilize during the

flowering: this is a basic principle in growing roses. The ideal is to apply a fertilizer formulated for roses at the very beginning of spring to stimulate re-growth after pruning; then one month later, and again in later summer after the first flowering is over, to encourage repeat flowering. A long-lasting fertilizer applied at the beginning of April will also do the job.

weeds, keeps the soil fresh, and produces a surface layer of humus beneficial to the development of the roots.
A 4 inch (10 cm) deep layer of an organic mulch, such as pine needles, salt hay or shredded bark is excellent.
On the other hand, avoid using fresh-cut grass, which gives off heat as it decomposes. This can hurt the roots and risk

But it's not merely a question of how or when to water. While the lack of water gives the rose a sad appearance, too much water can asphyxiate its roots, especially if the soil is heavy and poorly drained. Add to this that excessive watering can wash away the soil's fertile elements.
So, rather than repeated shallow watering, give an ample quantity of water

23. Regularly aerate the soil
Working the soil at the base of the roses with a hoe or fork aerates and loosens up the soil so that water can penetrate it better.
One morning each month during the growing period, hoe the soil carefully, taking care not to damage the surface roots. And use this chance to rake in grains of fertilizer.

Fertilizer for roses is available in the form of granules (to spread) or a liquid (to spray). It contains magnesium, an important element that stimulates foliage and flowering.

21. Mulch the base of your rose
A layer of mulch at the base of your rose helps prevent the excessive evaporation of water, constricts the growth of

encouraging disease. Finally, always mulch on clean and weeded soil.

22. Water as needed
A good supply of water is necessary for roses, especially in the first year of planting. Later on, they better withstand periods of dryness, but the beauty, abundance and duration of their flowering depends greatly on the satisfaction of their need for water.

all at once, an inch or so, directly to the base of each plant. Create a basin in the soil beforehand. Water once a week on average, depending on the weather.
Soak with a classic garden hose or watering can if you have only a few roses. A network of soaker hoses is ideal for more numerous plants. Above all, avoid a sprinkler—it wets the leaves and promotes disease.

The aeration of the soil is crucial for rose bushes grown in beds, for climbers, and for roses in containers. Shrub roses, on the other hand, require much less time and effort, and always have a nice appearance, even when left to themselves. But as a whole, these roses have no scent. Their beauty is their exuberant wild flowering throughout the summer.

24. Prune for good shape

Pruning a rose regularly each year allows you to balance the bush and keep the wood strong, from as close as possible to the ground. This is the making of a beautiful shrub.

In general, a vigorous rose bush should be pruned lighter; less hardy ones should be pruned heavier. It's the same for shrubs: the strong branches are depending on your climate, when the risk of heavy frost has passed.

25. Prune for good flowering

Don't hesitate to shorten the branches when pruning the roses, even if it seems you have nothing left. If too many buds remain, flowering branches will develop: their stems will be less vigorous and their flowers this keeps the rose from draining itself by forming buds, while renewing its vigor to continue flowering. With a grouped-flower rose bush, cut about 10 inches (25 cm) below the inflorescence. On a rose that doesn't repeat flower, pruning is generally done after the flowering between July and September, guaranteeing a neat appearance until the next year.

ous varieties can grow to 17–20 feet (5–6 m) in height and cover large surfaces.

Consider letting some floral branches softly fall to give a more romantic appearance.

Keep in mind that climbers left in "natural form" can grow wild to fill a large space in the center of a field.

pruned a bit lighter than the thinner branches.

The cut should be made at a slant about an eighth of an inch above a bud facing the outside of the cluster: first cut the dead wood, and then the poorly placed branches at the center of the shrub, as well as the weak branches. Then reduce by two-thirds some of the healthy and vigorous branches spreading out from the base of the plant. Prune in late winter, will be smaller. Unfortunately, there is no strict formula for the precise number of buds to leave: it depends upon species, observation, and aesthetics.

Good tools are a must. They must cut the stems cleanly at an angle to avoid a drop of water standing on the cut or risking the onslaught of disease.

Remove the wilted blooms throughout the flowering:

26. Attend to climbing roses

Unlike other climbing plants, the rose doesn't naturally produce a structure for hanging on, such as suckers or aerial roots. It needs your help. Throughout its growth, attach the stems with short, flexible ties to the surface on which it will grow—the uprights of a pergola or arch, the wall, the wire fence, or trellis. Some particularly vigor-

27. Remove the suckers

Suckers are the wonderfully healthy shoots that emerge from the base or the edge of a rose bush; they are generally very thorny and easily recognizable by the greater number of their leaflets, normally seven instead of five.

These are growths from the graft that have formed below the graft union and emerged from the soil. These healthy shoots draw considerable energy, and they will never flower. So cut them promptly, as close as possible to their point of origin. And don't forget a good pair of gloves!

To avoid the suckers in the first place, be sure the point of graft (the bud union) is not buried. And consider laying the rose bare at the end of winter, i.e., removing the small mound of earth that you some constraints. Strongly correlated to climate, fungus proliferates when the air is humid, with or without heat. Under the circumstances, it is always prudent to treat preventively: use a fungicide especially for roses. Treating in autumn, before the fall of the leaves, is also a wise precaution.

To limit the risks, adhere limit damage, at the very least.

Three diseases are the nemesis of roses: mildew, whose first symptom is a drying out of the young leaves before a white powder covers the stems, leaves and floral buds; rust, which manifests as small orange pustules on the underside of the leaves; and black spot, which presents as brown, blackish or purplish spots

30. Aphid control

Aphids, which appear in spring, invade the young shoots and then the floral buds, in colonies. They feed on the sap and weaken the plant, and they can carry disease, especially viruses.

Certain predators, such as ladybugs, can slow their growth, but in the case of heavy infestation there is little choice but recourse to insecticide.

put in place before the frost to protect the graft, the most sensitive part of the rose.

28. Prevent disease

In the foregoing portraits, you will have noticed that each rose has a varying degree of resistance to disease. Choosing the more resistant varieties, of course, may help assure success, but perhaps you have fallen for a color or a fragrance that comes with to a few rules: don't group or plant roses too close to each other as they tend to transmit diseases quickly. Plant a sensitive rose in relative isolation, at least 6.5 feet (2 m) away from its neighbors: the empty space is good, of course, for other kinds of plants.

29. Care for sick roses

An ounce of prevention is worth a pound of cure, of course. But sometimes cure works too. You can on the leaves.

If you haven't taken preventive action, you can still stop the disease at the appearance of the first symptoms and prevent it from overtaking the entire plant with the help of a chemical treatment. There are many name-brand specialty sprays for leaves. But those parts already infected are irremediably lost—you must eliminate them.

Technology, legislation and improved manufacturing have made the products available much easier to use, and they contain less aggressive active materials, while preserving effectiveness. They are available in liquid form to dilute with water and apply with a sprayer or ready-to-use; the latter is very practical if there are only a few roses to treat.

31. Eliminate red spider mites

Invisible to the naked eye, red spider mites—in fact, generally yellow—are detected through the discoloration of the leaves: they become grayish.

These tiny members of the class containing spiders, ticks and mites proliferate throughout the summer when the weather is warm and dry; they feed upon the cell fluids in the leaves, which then dry up and fall off.

Climbing roses growing on a very sunny wall protected from rain by an overhang are especially at risk. A chemical treatment is the only way to eliminate spider mites if their obvious presence risks damaging the general appearance of the rose. The preparation is sold in liquid form to be applied with a sprayer.

32. Treat your roses during winter

Winter or end-of-winter treatment products destroy fungal spores, and the eggs and larvae of aphids, scale, and caterpillars. Use them only on dormant shrubs, after they have shed their leaves. Essentially, these products are insecticide suspended in mineral oil. They eliminate the hibernating ravagers and prevent their return in the spring. Apply them with a sprayer.

This will significantly reduce the risk of insects and disease at the start of spring.

Bordeaux mixture can also be sprayed in winter. This traditional specialty product, with a base of copper, protects the flowers and fruit against a number of diseases, especially mildew, whose symptoms are often confused with those of black spot: both cause the appearance of black spots. But this is quite rare with garden roses: it occurs most often in greenhouses.

33. Treat chlorosis

Roses perform best in a slightly acidic soil with a pH between 5.5 and 6.5. In high alkaline soils with a pH around 7.0–7.5, roses have a tendency to develop chlorosis. This condition causes a discoloration of the leaf blades, while the veins remain nearly green: the presence of chalk prevents the plant from properly assimilating iron, one of the trace elements in soil, which operates in the synthesis of chlorophyll. You can combat this deficiency by applying a solution containing chelated iron once a month when watering the base of the rose from April to September. Sequestrene, or soluble trace elemental salts, is available in most nurseries.

You can also try lowering the pH of the soil by digging a small trench completely around your rose and refilling it with known acid soil mixed with original soil in autumn.

34. Remove wilted flowers

Unless you want to keep the decorative fruits of certain varieties through winter, you should remove wilted flowers. The flowers of many old varieties remain attached and develop into ugly gray balls, either dried up or full of water. In any case, they are unsightly, so remove them, if only for aesthetics. Other varieties graciously drop

their wilted petals, which nicely speckle the ground and leave the shrub clean and tidy.

By cutting the wilted blooms of repeat flowering varieties, you also prevent the plant from exhausting itself by forming fruit and restore its energy to continue flowering. Be sure to wear gloves and, with a pruning shears, cut the stem below the wilted flower,

The second type is clustered, inflorescenses of from five to six to as many as a dozen flowers; this is typical of grouped-flowering bushes, at one time called Floribunda or Polyantha. These forms flower longest and most prolifically.

On certain varieties of large-flowered rose bushes, the principle bud is surrounded by small side buds: remove them

keep them clear.

There are special herbicides for roses too; they help keep the soil free of extraneous vegetation. These are generally granules spread on clean soil at the beginning of spring to prevent the germination of undesirable plants.

If a bit of wild vegetation has sprung up around your roses, pull them out by hand with as much as

and buds—unless you want to keep the fruit for their decorative appearance in the winter.

Shorten by one-third the most vigorous stem branches, on average about 20 inches (50 cm) above the soil. You will thus reduce the bare branches to a neat little plant, which better resists the cold and wind of winter. If your roses form a hedge, simply trim the

above the first well-formed leaf with five leaflets.

35. De-bud the roses

Rose bushes exhibit two types of flowering.

The first is characterized by isolated flowers at the tip of the stem or joined with others, five or six at most: this is the flowering of large Hybrid Tea and Grandiflora bushes, among which are found most fragrant roses.

by hand or with a pruning shears to give greater energy to the principle flower. This is most important for roses grown for cutting.

36. Keep the soil clean

Keeping the soil clean around roses suppresses the competition of other plants for water and nutrition in the soil. Even if you grow your roses with other plants, hoe their bases regularly to

possible of their roots, and then treat the area to avoid re-growth.

If you choose not to use chemical products, weed the base of the roses regularly with a hoe.

37. Clean up at the end of the season

Once the flowering has ended, cut back all dead or broken branches, portions of stems still bearing faded flowers, and the undeveloped fruit

dead wood and the too-entangled branches.

All cuttings should be burned: they take much too long to decompose for compost and they risk preserving insect larvae and fungal spores.

38. Protect your roses from heavy frosts

Most varieties are hardy and can tolerate winter conditions. Prepare them all the same, to minimize the risk.

The graft point is the part of the rose most sensitive to cold. You can easily protect it by creating a mound beginning in autumn, covering it with a good 5 inches (12 cm) of soil. But don't forget to remove this mound when spring arrives to prevent the growth of all those pesky suckers.

Wrap the base and center of the rose bush with straw or some similar

39. Pick the flowers at the right moment

Pick roses early in the morning or after sunset, when they are slightly opened buds. Use flower cutters or pruning shears. Cut the stems about 12 to 16 inches (30–40 cm) in length, but no more, so as to permit the rose to flower quickly once again. If your roses are very thorny, remove the thorns as much as possible with

and if you leave your flowers for a few hours to absorb this liquid, you will minimize the trauma of the cut. The stems will eventually be cut again with a neat clean bevel.

40. Create a beautiful bouquet

Arrange the bouquet in your favorite vase. Again, remember to use a floral preservative to prolong the life and beauty of your

original sensation.

For more contrast, mix roses with other flowers and foliage—but always keep them in a proportion of at least three-quarters: the roses are the stars of the show.

41. Prolong the life of cut roses

The warmer the room where you place your bouquet, the more quickly the roses will open. Keep

insulating material, and attach it so that the wind doesn't blow it away.

With standard roses, the point of graft is some 10 inches (25 cm) above the ground, and this part must be protected. Non-woven winter insulation netting is an excellent solution. Two or three times in the course of winter, when the weather is nice and dry, open up the material and let the rose get air.

a good pair of scissors or a special tool. This will both prevent injury to you and the tangling of the flower stems in the arrangement. Remove the leaves on the bottom two-thirds of the stem.

Then plunge the stems immediately in room-temperature water to which has been added a cut floral preservative. This preservative contains both nutritious elements and antibacterial agents,

flowers.

Any container will do perfectly. And think about accessories: floral moss, flower picks, glass marbles, wire mesh.

Go wild with shape and color, but exercise the least restraint: try not to clash.

Some find a single fragrant variety is plenty for a whole bouquet. Others like to blend perfumes and practice alchemy among them, creating an

them in a cool place in order to conserve them. Remove wilted roses from the bouquet immediately. Just as one rotten apple spoils the bunch, a faded flower contaminates the others: it emits the gases of decomposition.

Flowers that are fading can sometimes be revived. Dip the end of the stem in boiling water to dilate its fibers, then cut off a quarter of an inchand dip immediately in cool water. This "electroshock" generally restores their vigor for a few days. You can also wrap the stems in stiff paper their entire length and place them in cool water for a few hours, just until the flowers have regained some freshness.

42. Rejuvenate an old rose

The purchase of an older home, a newfound passion, a visit to a friend's home necessary. Cut them at the base with a heavy-duty pruning shears, a two-handed pruning shears, or a handsaw; this will encourage the growth of new shoots. The following year, continue the structural renovation with another one or two old branches until you achieve complete renewal.

For a climbing rose, detach it completely to and it can be a nuisance: there are no fewer than 10,000 varieties catalogued!

To identify a variety with certainty, the rose in question (reproduced by cutting or grafting) must be planted next to named varieties to which it seems most similar. By a long process of observation and comparison, you can make the most accurate identification. And even moistened and protected. Layering is best suited for large rose shrubs rather than for large-flowered rose bushes. In layering, a branch is bent down during the growth period and buried approximately 6 inches (15 cm) so that it will take root.

Grafting is the method most generally used by commercial rose growers; it gives the best results and it's very workable for

where the garden is neglected…and there you find an old abandoned rose. It calls for your attention, needing only proper care and maintenance to flower plentifully next year.

Do a simple clean-up trim in winter, to eliminate dead branches and make a start on the rehabilitation. At the beginning of spring, perform a true maintenance pruning, removing one or two large old branches if aerate it fully, and then prune and retrain it.

43. Identify an unknown rose

Sometimes you need only kneel down to find an easily legible label at the base of a rose. But not very often….

While most people are content to admire their beauty and their fragrance, others must name and classify their roses. This takes time and effort this is no guarantee! Of course, there's always DNA….

44. Multiply your roses yourself

There are three procedures for multiplying roses, and any passionate enthusiast can do them. Propagation means taking 6-inch (15 cm) cuttings of branches in autumn and planting them in an adequate mixture of sand, peat, and garden soil, well amateurs. It is carried out in spring and consists of slipping a bud from the variety to be propagated (also known as the scion) under the bark of the branch of the understock and then securing it with a tight bond.

45. Hybridize your roses

You might be tempted to try hybridizing your own varieties of roses. And why not? Though your chances of discovering a pearl are minimal, there is untold satisfaction in the mere crossing, seedling, and creating of a new plant. Each parent brings its own genetic heritage: the "father," from which you take the pollen, generally contributes color and fragrance, while the "mother," whose flower you pollinate, usually transmits the qualities of vegetation.

a pot, replant the small saplings in a larger pot come spring…and await your first flowers.

46. Prepare a rose pot-pourri
There are many ways to make a pot-pourri. Here's a particularly easy one: Use fragrant varieties of roses, and pick the flowers when they are fully bloomed, right before they wither.

your mixed petals. The fragrances will blend wonderfully.
Finish the top with whole dried flowers.
Don't place pot-pourri in direct sunlight; it will fade the colors.

47. Use rose petals in cooking
The flowers bring to cooking a touch of poetry that alters everything….
Here are two easy recipes:

whites in a bowl. Dip the fragrant rose petals to moisten them, then sprinkle them with granulated sugar. Place them in a warm oven for about fifteen minutes, until they dry. Done!
Rose petals are also lovely decorations: red petals atop a salad or dessert will tempt both eyes and mouth.

Begin by removing the petals and the stamen of the rose you wish to hybridize. With a paintbrush, remove the pollen from the "father" rose and place it in the center of the bare flower, on the stigma. Cover this pollinated flower with a small bag to shield it from wind and insects. The success of the operation will manifest in autumn as a round fruit. Then you need only sow the seeds in December in

Remove the petals and place them on a hand towel in a well-ventilated, dry, and shady place to remove all moisture.
Feel free to mix as many species and varieties as you like to make a nice assortment of colors, sizes, shapes, and scents. Place a layer of petals in a glass jar and allow it to settle. Add a layer of dry leaves of eucalyptus or a layer of cinnamon sticks before another layer of

a rose wine that will surprise and delight your guests, and crystallized rose petals.
For rose wine, mix 8 ounces (250g) of fragrant, dried ground rose petals with a third of a quart of wine. Let it steep for 24 hours in the refrigerator. Pass it through a strainer and add the remaining two thirds of a quart of wine. Serve chilled.
For crystallized rose petals, mix two egg

48. Prepare a rose jam
In making rose preserves, you have a choice: use the flower's fruit, also known as rose hips, or its tender petals.
For a fruit jam, pick the fruit—the best varieties being *Rosa rugosa*—at their maturity, once they have taken on a nice orange color. Place them in boiling water for one hour, in order to open them and release the small inedible seed grains.

Open them before cooking and de-seed them by scraping the pulp. Once they are cooked, mash the fruits into a puree and mix them with crystallized sugar (2 cups per pound of crushed fruit) and the juice of one lemon. Let this simmer for thirty minutes after it returns to boiling.

With the petals of fragrant roses you can make a jelly: prepare a mar-

preserving both their color and perfume quite well. The only imperative: *dry the roses quickly, immediately after picking.* Choose completely dry flowers in dry weather (with no humidity or rain or dew), and keep only the most perfect specimens; the tiniest faults will be much more apparent after drying.

Remove the large leaves that wither in the drying.

bouquet, which can be preserved for years. You can regularly refresh the fading perfume with a couple drops of essential oil.

50. Photograph your roses

Is there a flower more photogenic than the rose? You may not be able to preserve your roses' sweet perfume all winter, but you can surely enjoy

Choose a sunny day for optimal lighting, and the morning hours, when the roses are most fresh.

Put your camera on a tripod for perfect clarity and use a film of ASA 100, for more sharpness and better definition of details.

With a telephoto lens, concentrate on isolated roses, but take in surrounding clusters. Avoid wide shots: the individual flowers will be too small

malade with 4.5 pounds of pears, pass it through a sieve, add five 2 cups of sugar per pint and about 8 ounces of dried petals.

49. Keep a bouquet of dried flowers

This is particularly good for fragrant flowers,

Then hang the floral stems upside down, individually or tied in groups, in a very dry, shady, well-ventilated area. Group no more than four or five flowers in a bunch or they may spoil. After a week the roses are ready to arrange in a

the sight of them in a frame or on the screen. And you can share your pride and pleasure, too, as greeting cards. Whether your subject is a single flower in a pot or a garden full of roses, a few rules apply to take the best photos.

and they become merely a disordered pattern.

Contents

Index

[Glossary]

Black spot: fungal disease manifesting as black spots that appear on the leaves.

Bud: first stage of the flower, when the petals are still closed upon themselves, before blooming.

Corolla: part of the flower formed by the petals, often very colorful.

Cup: the flower is more or less hollow, with very large outer petals, concave at the base and curled on the top edge, resembling the shape of a cup.

Enriching agents: substances incorporated into the soil to improve the physical and chemical composition.

Evergreen: tree that doesn't lose its leaves in winter.

Leaflet: each division of the lamina of the composite leaf. The serration of the leaflets can be small or large.

Mildew: fungal disease manifesting as a deformation of leaves and a white covering that invades the entire plant little by little.

Mutation: variation that appears suddenly in the lineage of a plant and that cannot be used to create a new variety.

Peduncle: stem of a flower or fruit.

Perennial: plant that grows back year after year thanks to its genetic composition.

Preventive treatment: a treatment applied to a plant before it is diseased in order to prevent any attacks.

Quarter: in the center of a quartered rose, the petals are distinctly divided into 4 or 5 groups that curve inwards towards each other.

Repeat flowering: type of flowering which spreads itself out over the entire season, either in a continuous fashion from spring to autumn, or interrupted, with a break during the hottest part of the summer.

Rosette: ensemble spread out in a circle.

Rust: fungal disease manifesting as small orange and then black spots on the leaves.

Scrolled: literally shaped like a top. A bud whose petals are prettily overlapped on each other.

Shape of the flower: a simple rose has only 5 petals. Semi-double, it has 2 to 5 rows of petals. Double, it has still more, naturally letting the stamen be seen. The petals of a semi-full rose must actually be uncurled by hand to see them. A full rose presents a compact mass of petals, with the stamen seeming totally absent.

Stamen: male reproductive organ of plants and flowers, formed by a thin part, the filament, and a bulbous part, the anther, which encloses the pollen.

Sucker: volunteers that grow from the graft and not from the cultivated variety.

Train: attach parts of the plant, stems and branches, to a support to keep them growing in the desired direction.

[Photo Credits]

All photos are by Jacques Boulay with the exception of:
p. 2: Marc Walter
p. 4/5: Marc Walter
p. 6: Marc Walter
p. 9: B. Clarisse-Pichon (Geswind Schouste)
p. 11, 12,13: Marc Walter
p. 14 (bottom): B. Clarisse-Pichon (Roseraie de L' Haÿ)
p. 15: B. Clarisse-Pichon (Express of China)
p. 17: (bottom) Marc Walter
p. 17: Hachette (top)
p. 20: Hachette (top)
p. 22: Marc Walter
p. 25: Marc Walter
p. 26: Hachette (bottom left)
p. 26: B. Clarisse-Pichon (top right, Jardins de Vieilles-Maisons)
p. 27, 28: Marc Walter
p. 29: Le Scanff-Mayer (Roseraie de Blois)
p. 30, 31: (Julie Delbard) B. Clarisse-Pichon (left)
p. 35: B. Clarisse-Pichon
p. 43: B. Clarisse-Pichon
p. 48: B. Clarisse-Pichon
p. 70: DEVD 94/D. Petit
p. 71: B. Clarisse-Pichon (Roseraie de Berty)
p. 73, 74, 75, 77, 78, 84, 85: B. Clarisse-Pichon
p. 87: J.- P. Guillot
p. 93, 94: B. Clarisse-Pichon
p. 96: Guillot
p. 97: B. Clarisse-Pichon
p. 99: Guillot
p. 101: B. Clarisse-Pichon (Jardins de Vieilles-Maisons)
p. 104: Le Scanff-Mayer (Roses anciennes, André Eve)
p. 106, 119, 120,121: B. Clarisse-Pichon
p. 123: Delbard
p. 125: Delbard
p. 127: Le Scanff-Mayer (Jardins des paradis, Cordes sur ciel)
p. 129: B. Clarisse-Pichon
p. 133: B. Clarisse-Pichon
p. 137: NIRP
p. 140: Delbard
p. 145: B. Clarisse-Pichon (left)
p. 147: B. Clarisse-Pichon, (third from the left, Roseraie de L' Haÿ)

[Acknowledgments]

Yves le Floc' h Soye, Marie-Hélène Loaëc et Jacques Boulay thank : The Department of Parks, Gardens and Outdoors in Paris, The Department of Outdoors and the Society for Improvement and Development in Nantes, which allowed us to use reports from the École du Breuil, the Parc de Bagatelle, the Roseraie du Val-de-Marne, and the Roseraie du Parc de La Beaujoire.
For their extremely important help, we would like to thank André Brunei, Aline Converset, Bernard Mando, Raymond Nazereau and Alain Woisson, rose growers Michel Adam, Henri Delbard, André Eve, Jean-Pierre Guillot, Monique Laperriére, Alain Meilland, and Pierre Orard, perfume makers René Cornon and Jean-F. Laporte as well as Mr. Petit, the nurserymen Loubert, Mr. Brunel, Mr. Franchellin, Marie-Hélène Leduc, Vincent Motte, Gilles Le Scanff and Joëlle-Caroline Mayer, Béatrice Pichon-Clarisse and Nikoleta Nikolova.

Jardin des Sens series editior: Yves le Floch'h Soye
Translation: Kim Allen

Library of Congress Cataloging-in-Publication Data Available

1 3 5 7 9 10 8 6 4 2

Published by Sterling Publishing Company, Inc.
387 Park Avenue South, New York, N.Y. 10016
Originally published in France under the title *Jardin des Sense: Roses* and © 2000 by Hachette Livre (Hachette Pratique)
English translation © 2002 by Sterling Publishing Co., Inc.
Distributed in Canada by Sterling Publishing
c/o Canadian Manda Group, One Atlantic Avenue, Suite 105
Toronto, Ontario, Canada M6K 3E7
Distributed in Great Britain and Europe by Cassell PLC
Wellington House, 125 Strand, London WC2R 0BB, England
Distributed in Australia by Capricorn Link (Australia) Pty. Ltd.
P.O. Box 704, Windsor, NSW 2756 Australia

Printed in Singapore
All rights reserved

Sterling ISBN 0-8069-7301-3